Becoming
Plumb
Healthy

For David & Ilene
So you can see how I put it all together
Enjoy!
Herb Potash
(DOCTOR P)

Becoming Plumb Healthy

Herbert M. Potash

Gordon Handwerk Publishers
Madison, New Jersey
Midland, Michigan
Wilmington, Delaware

Production: Stephanie Barry
Cover Design: Andrew Burd
Typeface: Garamond
Printer: Cushing-Malloy, Ann Arbor, MI

Library of Congress Cataloging-in-Publication Data

Potash, Herbert M.
Becoming plumb healthy / by Herbert M. Potash.
p. cm.
Includes bibliographical references.
ISBN 0-940524-06-6 (pbk.)
1. Existential psychology. I. Title.
BF204.5.P68 2005
150.19'52--dc22

2005027887

Acknowledgments

Many people influenced my writing this book. Existential philosophers and psychologists were the beginning point for much of my thinking; and although I do directly acknowledge specific books, certainly other unnamed authors also affected my views. Students, most particularly in my existential psychology classes, helped me refine and further develop my thinking through their questions. Ongoing discussions with psychotherapy clients were crucial for discovering the most helpful strategies leading individuals to fuller psychological health.

Helpful suggestions for modifications of the text were given by Kathy Conroy and Tony Tasso. My daughter Stephanie Barry not only made suggestions for improving the text but also arranged final production. Andrew Burd designed the cover of the book, created the web pages for Gordon Handwerk Publishers and arranged for internet distribution and publication.

Most importantly, my wife and lifetime partner Jan is most responsible for shepherding this book into its final form. She made many helpful suggestions which helped refine my thinking, beginning with the initial first draft and extending through the final copy. Her editorial skills have made the book much more readable. I am and forever will be grateful for all of her assistance in making it possible for me to be a successful academician, psychotherapist and author.

Dedicated to

Sam, Max, William, Nicky and Michael

With love from Doc

TABLE OF CONTENTS

Prologue

In the same year I accepted early retirement from my position as a university professor, my eldest grandchild entered kindergarten. The fact that these two events occurred in the same year was a major motive leading me to begin work on this book. I felt that I wanted to be able to share relevant parts of my professional life with my grandchildren. Obviously, when a grandparent spends time with grandchildren who are toddlers or school age, the fact that the grandparent is a college professor and psychotherapist cannot be of any particular interest to the children. Instead, the relationship revolves around play and upon the comfortable, easy love and sharing that occurs across these generations. I have been able to simply enjoy myself with these children without my academic or professional self needing to make an appearance. At certain times when the grandchildren visited our home, I did have to work in my office, seeing psychotherapy clients; but the children never gave that much attention. What those appointments simply meant for them was that they had to be quiet and could not play in the living room.

My grandchildren know me as being one kind of person, and I hoped that in the future when they were adults, they could discover another side of me through reading this book. All of us show different sides of ourselves to different people. As the first American psychologist, William James, said, we act and feel in quite different ways with each of the people we spend time with. When we are lovers we function quite differently from when we are being sons or daughters or co-workers or friends.

In my professional life, I have functioned in various capacities, yet all of these jobs allowed me to try to make a positive difference in the ways people functioned. I have had a lengthy career as a clinical psychologist which involved being a university professor, engaging in research and conducting psychotherapy. As a psychotherapist, I have counseled a number of people, helping them gain a better understanding of themselves. My clients have used these insights to find the strength to face and overcome their difficulties. As an academician, I taught graduate students both how to effectively treat and to assess their own psychotherapy patients. After leaving academia, I continued to train and assist psychotherapists by providing clinical supervision to different mental health professionals.

However, one regret I do have is not being able to again offer the course in existential psychology I developed and taught for many years. I have repeatedly been told by countless students how they used this information to make important changes in their lives. A number of years ago I had turned to the writings of existentialists to help me cope with the grief I felt over the death of my mother. The existentialists consider it imperative to be able to confront one's own mortality and to use that knowledge to create one's own unique approach to life. In time I realized that I would best understand these writings if I taught a course in existential psychology. I had previously discovered that to give an effective lecture, I needed to have a deeper level of understanding than one obtained from simply reading a theory. I revised my approach to teaching the existential course over the years and showed the students how these ideas could be made personally meaningful in order to assume better control over their lives. As a teacher I drew upon my insights as a therapist to demonstrate how the more abstract philosophical ideas could be given very real practical application to everyday living.

My experience providing therapy enabled me to apply these existential concepts to concrete situations. As a graduate student, I was drawn to existential ideas but I viewed many of the texts as obscure and overly intellectualized. I found the writings of existential philosophers particularly difficult; and while I still am not sure that I fully understand these authors, I realize that many other psychologists have been just as confused as I was. In fact, most psychologists do not see any positive uses for existential concepts and, therefore, do not use these ideas in their therapeutic practice. Many people misunderstand existential ideas; furthermore, even different mental health professionals who call themselves "existential" interpret these writings very differently.

As a young adult undergoing graduate school training, I wanted to develop a meaningful professional identity, but I also felt it was imperative to decide how best to direct my personal life. Even though I discovered that some of my personal and professional views echoed the ideas of existential philosophers, I nonetheless very much needed to be my own person. I have always inwardly rebelled against being an *ist* because when you are an *ist,* your individuality is diminished by the use of a label, be it psychologist, psychotherapist, existentialist, artist, or any other category one ascribes to. I was not and still am not in full agreement with all the existential writings, and most particularly, I disagree with the ways that many existentialists believe psychotherapy should be conducted. I strongly endorse the position that effective psychotherapy is very much an intimate, caring relationship. I know that it is through this relationship that people find the strength to conquer their problems. I also consider it vitally important for therapists to be able to respond to people in many different ways. The therapist must be able to complement the client's different needs which means that sometimes the therapist has to be very quiet while at other times, directive. These ideas alone set me apart from other therapists who use the label "existentialist" to describe their approach.

I presented my ideas about how to understand and treat the serious problems people face in my book, *Pragmatic-existential psychotherapy with personality disorders* (1994). Although I wrote the book primarily for psychotherapists in training, some of my clients have also read the book and found these ideas very helpful in coping with their own difficulties.

A major theme I presented in that book was that all people have a basic need to develop in healthy directions and to continue to move their lives forward in productive and meaningful ways. Simultaneously, we all have unhealthy tendencies, and people who are in a great deal of psychological pain can be described as dominated too much by their unhealthy sides. Effective therapy, then, becomes viewed as an alliance between the therapist and the healthy side of the client's personality.

My initial intent in writing this current book was to present the central ideas of the existential psychology course in practical terms that will be useful for my grand-children as they enter college. Because I have known that young adults are especially receptive to these ideas, I hope that through the book I can communicate to the students with whom I would otherwise not have the opportunity to explain and discuss these important life affirming ideas. Therefore, I acknowledge the book is not simply being written for five grandchildren, but hopefully will also appeal to all about to undertake the journey toward adulthood.

Although the desire for greater self-understanding and insight initially appears in adolescence, it is not confined to that period in life. Particularly upon entering the mid-life years, many people find it especially important to reflect back upon their lives in order to better chart their future direction. The recognition of the value of increased self-awareness leads many people to seek books such as this one or to enter psychotherapy to enhance their level of self-understanding. This book is written to help satisfy such needs.

I have still another audience in mind for this book. My work as a psychotherapist focuses upon solving the particular problems that each client faces. In therapy sessions we only need to discuss the life issues that present emotional difficulties and do not need to address those areas where the client already demonstrates strengths. Therefore, one may discuss anger with one client, identity issues with a second, and sexuality with a third. Rarely do I speak about all areas of functioning with all clients. By writing this book I am able to systematically address a method of approaching life in its totality through a forum that allows me to develop many of my ideas.

In the existential psychology classroom, I only could discuss human struggles in the abstract as it was inappropriate to turn the class into a group psychotherapy session. In the consulting room, however, I certainly can discuss the relevant issues for each client but our discussions are primarily restricted to the problematic issues. In writing this book I am, therefore, engaged in a process similar to teaching a new course. I have attempted to put my thoughts together in a systematic way that makes my ideas more coherent and consistent. Also, and perhaps most importantly, this book has been written to communicate to the healthy and growth-seeking side of the reader's personality, no matter what your age, in the hopes that it will strengthen your ability to counteract any unhealthy tendencies.

Consequently, this book has been written for everyone interested in exploring the question *How can I better understand myself and best approach my life?* Some potential readers with a particular intellectual bent can view the text as offering an understanding of the practical applications of existential themes to everyday living. Finally, if my wishes do come true, my grandchildren eventually will also read this book.

On The Perils of Beginning

I spent far too much time and energy thinking about the best way to start and organize this book. Some days I initially felt quite pleased about what I had written; but when I would return to the computer and reread my sentences, I often found them unclear or redundant or in strong need of rewriting. I simply could not find the best or right way to present the different topics that I wanted to discuss. As I continued to mull over different possible beginnings, I was reminded of a character described in Camus' novel *The Plague* (1993). Camus wrote of an aspiring novelist, Joseph Grand, who kept polishing and rewriting the first sentence of his novel. Joseph was continually asking other people for their reactions to his newest first sentence. In his incessant search for the best opening sentence, Joseph Grand never allowed himself to write a second sentence.

This little vignette graphically reminds us of one of the many perils that we humans continually face. Joseph

Grand represents all of us in that he has a particular goal (in his case, to write a novel) and is very much invested in reaching that goal. We might even speculate that he had the type of school teacher who stressed the importance of writing a good topic sentence at the beginning of each paragraph. The fact that he was trying so hard to find the right start for his novel seems to be commendable. Because he knew that he could improve on his work product, it is certainly quite understandable that Grand would put a lot of energy into such striving for excellence. If, in fact, we humans did not think that we could do better tomorrow than we have done today, we would no longer have goals to strive for. When we no longer believe in our capacity to improve ourselves, we quickly become subject to serious depression.

Our desire to improve our work efforts would seem to signify that we have strong motivation, that we are positively invested in ourselves and in our future, and that we have sufficiently high self-esteem to believe in ourselves and our capabilities. With such high task involvement, there is no good reason to settle for a second rate performance. Not to want to do the best possible job makes one sound like a "slacker." People with high task involvement may very well have a "fear of failure" and do not want to confess to laziness or low motivation. Instead, they need to see themselves as dedicated, hard working and invested in their work and their lives.

However, for some people, the desire to perform in the best possible manner can become transformed into a highly destructive motive instead of representing a lofty and important goal. The transformation of *wishes* from healthy motives into unhealthy *demands* can happen quite subtly. It is in part a consequence of the fact that whenever we become engaged in problem-solving activities, we often are able to discover which are the better and which are the worse ways of doing things. Our success in finding better strategies can lead us to the false conclusion that if we devote enough energy, we can ultimately find the best strategies for each potential action. It is extremely rare and usually impossible to discover the absolute best possible way of doing anything. If we tell ourselves that it is imperative to find the best way to proceed, we will set a trap for ourselves. We would be setting a goal for ourselves which would be impossible to reach. We need to come to terms with the truth that we are fallible human beings who must and will make mistakes.

The desire for perfection can function as a positive and worthwhile goal as long as we continue to recognize that true perfection is unattainable. If we demand of ourselves that we always act in the best way possible, we intuitively must also understand that we cannot uniformly know what is the best way possible. The unrealistic demand for perfection necessarily creates an inner tension with no mechanism present to provide relief from such stress. As a result, some people ultimately become immobilized because they fear acting in a wrong or deficient manner. Individuals who are caught in this destructive pattern often find or create particular rationalizations that perpetuate this dilemma. They tell themselves that they should neither settle for, nor accept, an inferior or less perfect way of action. This type of thinking places one on the same unproductive road that Joseph Grand traveled in *The Plague.*

My own struggle to find the best way to begin this book also reminded me of how I felt when I was preparing lecture notes for the initial meetings of the existential psychology course. There, too, I struggled to find the best way to present material until I ultimately found a solution. As a professor, it was necessary for me to remember that my students, just like all other people, would understand course content at different speeds of learning. The most basic ideas of existentialism can be immediately grasped by some students while others need to hear the material repeated in different ways before they begin to really understand these concepts. It was comforting to realize that the different paces of learning were functions of each student's intelligence, learning style and receptivity to the material. When some students looked at me with a blank stare, I assured myself that their lack of comprehension simply reflected they needed more repetition of the particular concept before they could incorporate it. Their difficulty in learning did not have to be attributed to deficient lectures. Of course, I also had to be open to the possibility that some of my lectures actually were unclear or poorly written, best noted if no one in the class appeared to understand what I was saying. On the other hand, when several class members nodded in agreement to what had just been discussed, I could conclude that my lecture was well understood even though other students appeared to be somewhat puzzled.

As a psychotherapist, I have also had to better understand why some of the things I have said to clients did not seem to register with them. I would make a point, or give an interpretation to a client, and reiterate it in different ways many times over. Again, some people only needed to hear an interpretation once before they immediately grasped its relevance. Other clients would describe, during a therapy session occurring weeks or months later, the remarkable insight they had just independently discovered. This new awareness would often be the same interpretation I had repeatedly made in earlier therapy sessions. One client helped me to understand this process in still a fuller way. He said the repeated iteration of a concept made small imperceptible inroads in his mind and he realized this repetition was necessary for his ultimate fuller self-awareness.

Certainly some of the difficulty I have had in being understood is a consequence of unclear communication. At other times, the simple truth is that some clients were not ready to hear particular interpretations because accepting these communications would mean facing difficult and painful truths. Therefore, effective communications with others is a complex matter, and misunderstandings can be a consequence of what is going on in both the speaker and the listener at that moment.

My problem deciding how to begin has its own particular history because I once was confused over the meaning of the word "commence." I was never sure if "commence" meant to begin or to end. Are the commencement exercises regularly held at graduations beginnings or endings?

When I finally consulted the dictionary to clear up my confusion, I found that the definition of commence means to begin. However, as I thought more about the meaning of the word "commence," I realized that the dictionary definition was in itself deficient. I had regularly confused beginnings with endings because I implicitly understood the validity of what is called dialectic reasoning. The major premise of dialectic reasoning is that we can only understand one concept because we know its opposite exists. In the specific case of commencement, we can only *begin* something by simultaneously *ending* something. To start anew is to let go of the old. However, that truth is very painful and uncomfortable for us to accept, and we regularly fight its validity. We do not want to have to give up anything in order to gain something new.

I have seen this dilemma so graphically with our dogs, Jasper and Lleucie. When they are holding treasures in their mouths and see another treasure, they face a major dilemma. They cannot put something new in their mouth without dropping whatever it is they are holding. We can all empathize with these dogs' dilemmas, because we, too, do not wish to have to make difficult choices that necessitate relinquishing anything. We want to be able to keep one foot in the old while we place our other foot into the new. This feeling is aptly summed up in the proverb of *You want to have your cake and eat it too.* Oh, that we could accomplish it!

When we have a strong musical talent, we may wish to be able to master the piano, guitar, drums and flute or even other instruments. However, whatever time we spend working on one instrument keeps us from being able to practice the other instruments. As a result, none of us can be a true expert on all instruments. If we spend the majority of our time practicing these musical instruments, then we cannot spend enough time attempting to master other activities. Therefore, whenever we start something new we must necessarily stop doing other things.

Each time I come to the computer in order to work on this book, I have to stop whatever else I have been doing. I continually begin and end doing things. Such changing activity is how we all lead our lives, through a series of ongoing beginnings and endings. Another way to describe this fact of life is to say that we are, indeed, all works in progress. For young adults, being a work in progress will usually feel very natural and the right state of affairs.

However, at ages 40 or 70 many people no longer want to be a work in progress but rather desire to be a long completed and well-defined entity. Because we are all human, we are continually engaged in beginnings and endings no matter what our ages happen to be. This truth, like virtually all the other truths discussed by existential writers, can be felt as being both an awful as well as a wonderful condition. To be able to improve on what we have already accomplished is very good. Yet, to recognize that what we have made of ourselves is still tentative and changeable can also be quite frightening. We need to allow ourselves both the good and bad feelings that come with the recognition of difficult truths about our human condition.

Most specifically, we need to understand that we do not create problems for ourselves simply because we are regularly beginning and ending activities. Such changes are a necessary part of the human condition. However, on different occasions we all may attribute specific and unnecessary meanings to these beginnings and endings and, at such times, we may create unnecessary stress and unhappiness for ourselves.

One such example would be when a man decides he would like to spend time with a woman he has recently met. He may consider approaching the woman and suggesting they spend some time together. If the man thinks that he would only like to discover if this is a relationship he would care to explore, then he should not have any particular difficulty in expressing his interest. However, if the man gives additional meanings to this potential encounter then it will become more difficult for him to speak to the woman.

Some men place themselves at risk whenever they approach a woman because they see her interest (or lack of interest) as a measure of their own personal worth. Consequently, as they express the desire to pursue relationships they place themselves in a vulnerable position. They have too much to lose if the women are uninterested in seeing them and, therefore, they are likely to avoid suggesting any encounter. There is no real objective risk in asking another person to spend time with you. However, potentially gratifying encounters can be transformed into painful experiences if the person places too much significance on the meeting.

Whenever we decide to stop doing one activity and to move to another, that decision need not be stressful in and of itself. We are capable of giving excessive meanings to our decision to change our course of action which, again, will make problems for ourselves. We can severely criticize ourselves for having abandoned the previous activity because of laziness or not spending enough time trying to master that particular task. On the other hand, we can tell ourselves that we are not ready for the "big step" that a new activity requires.

Again, it is how we view our particular situation and the meaning we give to changing that situation that can generate feelings of stress. We can see and interpret ourselves as being at so much significant risk with changes that this perception can keep us from being able to move forward with our lives. We will experience some feelings of loss whenever we engage in new beginnings, but the felt level of risk will be a consequence of how we view the significance of change.

The external events in our lives are not what typically cause us anxiety and pain. Rather, it is our interpretation of the significance of the situations that can make us very uncomfortable. For example, it is not unusual to be in disagreement with another person. Seeing things differently is not a problem unless we define it as a problem. If we tell ourselves that we must change the other person's position or that we cannot make any concessions to that person's opinion, then we have placed additional meaning onto the situation. We have added terms like "must" and "should" to what can transpire and therefore have added potentially far-reaching consequences to our dealings with other people. Whenever we tell ourselves that we must change the other person's opinion and are unable to do so, we are liable to launch into self-blame and self-attack. Making unrealistic or excessive demands upon oneself can only make trouble for ourselves.

We are always beginning something new even though the activity may be very similar to what we have done before. We never fully engage in the identical activity that we have done before. Getting up and going to class or to work on one Wednesday morning is different from getting up and going to class or to work on Tuesday morning because one more day has passed and one's outlook can and likely will change on the next day. If you wake up on a Wednesday morning and make a pronouncement such as *Today is the first day of my new life*, then you are approaching the day by focusing upon the likely possibility of making significant changes, which can either be uplifting or the source of new or additional stress. We all need to accept the fact that we continue to experience changes for we are continually beginning and ending. Change is inevitable and inescapable. Some changes will feel good and other changes will not. Even as we embrace the necessity of making changes in ourselves, we also need to protect ourselves from being over-invested in change. We cannot regularly and continually change in radical ways because that would be disorienting. We need to accept that it is natural to change and yet allow ourselves to undergo changes at a relatively comfortable pace.

To further explain my point, regard my writing this book. I am very invested in trying to make this into an excellent book. However, I need to recognize that whatever I am now writing I could rewrite endlessly. Furthermore, I could look at what I have written some five years in the future and know I would have been able to express my ideas in a much better fashion if I had written this book at a later point in time. I also need to recognize that I can always second guess myself. I can tell myself that I could always do better later because then I will have acquired more experience and knowledge than I now possess.

Nonetheless, if I wait for later to begin there will never be a beginning, just as was the case with Joseph Grand. I need to let myself write this book now, knowing that it is not the best of all possible books that I could write. I still want to make it the best book I can write now without demanding that it be perfect. Again, I must maintain high task involvement without letting myself become trapped in an incessant search for perfection. In short, this book can only represent a statement made by a particular work in progress, me, at this particular point in time.

I hope this book will have its own existence, that is, that it will actually be published, and will have a permanence that I personally cannot have. Many people reading these words may conclude that I take definitive positions about what I consider to be the better ways of approaching life. Their perceptions are indeed accurate. However, this book only can express the definiteness that I feel now at the time of this writing. I certainly expect that most of the ideas that I espouse will remain my ideas in the future, but I cannot be fully certain of this fact.

Perhaps you, my readers, may agree or disagree with what I am now saying but you very well may change your viewpoint at a later date. If that proves to be the case, then you will likely have read the book more than once. I certainly hope that you will do so because none of us totally grasp an idea the first time it is presented. Some ideas will feel very right when we first hear them. This kind of deep resonance is part of what I understand as *being plumb*, which I will explain more fully later in the book. Because we are all works in progress, we are not always immediately receptive; we need to give ourselves additional opportunities to comprehend new material. We cannot escape our human fallibility. The sooner we come to terms with our limitations, the less stressful our lives will become.

Being A Work In Progress

I view people basically as works in progress because this particular phrase captures two of the most crucial characteristics of our human condition. The first characteristic we exhibit, both to ourselves and to others, is a certain kind of stable consistency in our experience and behavior that persists over time. To make this point in the simplest of terms, we all stay the same. The second and seemingly contradictory characteristic is that we continue to change and evolve over time. Therefore, we both change and stay the same. If people were to continuously change without retaining any aspect of their past, they would have no core to themselves and would lack a stable sense of a self. They would live so continuously in the moment that they would lack the necessary tools to make good sense of what is actually happening in that moment. If each moment were totally new, we could not even use our language to understand the moment. Language is something we bring with us into a new situation; and if every moment were totally new, we would not have methods or ways to understand it. Similarly, we could not use our earlier experiences to help reach any understanding of the immediate present because knowing one's earlier experiences means drawing upon the past. In short, we would be totally nonfunctional if we were to approach every moment in our lives as a totally new and different experience.

On the other hand, if we retain a rigid belief in who we are and what the world is like, without being open to new experiences or learning, our lives will be so stale, repetitive and boring that they may lack meaning. We would not be able to develop a new approach to an old situation. We would be unwilling to change our ways of thinking or to learn from our past mistakes. If we were to spend our lives in this rigid mind set, we would be living as if we already knew everything, which is a blatant form of self-deception. On the other hand, if we approach life as if each moment is totally new, we would be living as if we knew nothing, which is another kind of self-deception.

Because neither extreme is true or possible, we are left with the basic truth that sometimes we change and sometimes we do not change. We change both in major and in minor ways. Some of these changes are quite apparent to others, while other changes are apparent only to ourselves. Some of the changes are a result of a deliberate use of our will, while some other changes simply seem to happen to us without any particular rhyme or reason. Still other changes in us are a direct consequence of the actions of others, and sometimes we may fail to notice that we have actually changed. We therefore are very complicated works in progress because many different forces lead us to change.

A simple example can illustrate that we are both open as well as resistant to change. Most of us relish the idea of taking a summer vacation, and many of us have a favorite place to return to, be it mountains, seashore or lake. Some of us believe that it would not seem like summer if we could not return to our favorite vacation place. The desire to keep returning to the same place to recapture the same experiences reflects a part of us that does not change.

On the other hand, we may also very much enjoy going to new places for vacation. The idea of seeing different things, eating exotic foods and having new experiences can be exciting. The desire to spread one's wings and to keep expanding the horizon is a natural expression of our need to grow and develop. If we did not look for new and different experiences when leaving home for the first time, then we would be confined to very narrow boundaries. However, if we never revisit the comfortable and familiar, we are cheating ourselves of some valuable experiences.

We feel a great deal of comfort in keeping or returning to the familiar especially when the familiar is rewarding. New experiences can also be very rewarding as well for they, too, further our sense of ourselves or our surroundings. We all need to find an effective balance between repeating familiar gratifying experiences where we do not significantly change, and allowing for new and rewarding experiences which can indeed produce change. Still, many of us struggle over vacation plans because we both want to revisit the old and to experience the new. Only a few lucky ones among us can afford to do both.

When we regularly embrace the new, we accelerate the process of change. I personally love to discover new things because they often alter and expand my perspectives, enabling me to see myself and others in a different light. When I discover a book by a new author whose ideas resonate with me, it is a wonderful experience. Reading such a book provides me with a different kind of validation which once again tells me to trust my own perceptions. In a similar manner, when I talk with interesting people I expand my knowledge and may even change some views of the world around me.

I remember reading that Socrates took a flute lesson on the day before his execution. When asked why he was doing so, his answer was quite life-affirming. He responded, *When else will I be able to take the lesson*? This anecdote has very important implications. It tells us that growth and change are possible until the moment of death. It is important to allow ourselves to keep finding and embracing new and potentially rewarding experiences. In that way we never really grow old as we can continue to find the excitement and wonder of life.

A person can be very old even when the calendar says that they are physically very young. "Old" means not changing and being "young," therefore, means being open to growth and change. It is not the objectively stated facts, such as age or time, that create our experiences. Rather, it is how we experience things that becomes our basic reality. There are moments when I very much am old and those are the times when my body aches. For example, when I spend several hours in the company of my grandchildren I may feel quite young, but often after they have gone home, I feel very old. My body reminds me that I must pay a high price for attempting to match children's activity levels. On the other hand, my eagerness to explore new things, to learn and to create are all activities that speak to my being young.

As we embrace the possibility of change it is important that we undergo change at a sensible pace to avoid feeling overwhelmed. I remember seeing an amusing movie several years ago that had the intriguing title *If it's Tuesday, this must be Belgium.* The movie described a whirlwind travel vacation where the characters visited a new country every day so that the continual, radical change of experiences proved dizzying. The movie title implicitly tells us that while we may need a particular mnemonic device to orient ourselves, there may be better ways to capture new experiences. If we are going to visit Belgium, or any other country, we need to do so at a pace where we can remember and digest what we have seen. If we have to consult the calendar to figure out where we are, then we are moving far too quickly to be able to enjoy ourselves.

We create change in ourselves in different ways. Often we institute changes simply through our behavior. Other times we change ourselves through our intellect and our experiences. The situations that we find ourselves in can often lead us to change. A host of different factors can produce change in ourselves; therefore, it is particularly important to try to understand more fully how we stay the same and how we change. The better we know ourselves, the more likely it is for us to be able to use this understanding and our will to direct desirable changes as we solidify the parts of ourselves that we hold dear and precious. If we do not attempt to monitor how and why of change and no change, we most likely will be controlled by chance and random external factors.

Perhaps an analogy will make this point clearer. As a work in progress, each human being can be likened to a collage. The different objects attached to the canvas of the collage consist of one's past experiences, one's thoughts, emotions and self-evaluations as well as the influences of other people. We humans are not just the canvas but we are also the artists who assemble and construct the collage. We are able to paint over parts of the canvas, add new elements and restructure the collage. On the other hand, we can also accept the collage as it exists in the moment and allow it to continue in an unaltered form. As I see it, we humans are all artists who can create and recreate the collage that is ourselves. However, before we can meaningfully decide how to change the collage and make it more functional or beautiful, we first must carefully study the collage that exists at this moment. When we allow ourselves to objectively evaluate the collage, we will be able to see which parts of us are right and which are discordant and need to be changed. This is the challenge we face if we are to forge a successful and meaningful personal life.

I strongly believe that self-study and self-understanding enable us to create a more fulfilling life because it allows us to see the possibilities of change. I am sure that I gravitated toward a career as a psychotherapist and a teacher because I especially believed in heightened self-awareness and in personal growth. Although a profound interest in self-understanding does not necessarily propel one to become a healing professional, a high level of self-understanding is certainly indispensable among psychotherapists if they are to perform their jobs well. However, introspection and a willingness to change oneself are the key ingredients for exerting control and mastering the direction of one's life, whatever one's occupation.

Self-exploration is not always a pleasant process. It can generate dread and despair, but it can also produce exhilaration and the feeling of heightened personal power. Many people find the best way to engage in self-exploration is through entering personal psychotherapy. Having spent a professional lifetime assisting others as a psychotherapist, I know of the positive power and value of psychotherapy when it is practiced by a skilled professional. On the other hand, I also recognize that psychotherapy is not the panacea for all human problems, and many people do not need the assistance of a therapist. Nonetheless, we can all profit from ongoing self-exploration and whatever the method, the process must begin by oneself with oneself.

Many people find it quite difficult to evaluate themselves and their situations objectively. They are often hypercritical, and when they engage in self-analysis it can quickly deteriorate into self-attack. Anyone who regularly feels victimized by such self-criticism will not profit from self-evaluation. In this situation such a person will need the assistance of a therapist who will help make the evaluation process more rational, leading to significant positive personal changes.

Some of us are lucky or graced enough to find a partner, peer or lover who can be a valuable sounding board when we engage in self-study. When we talk about ourselves to a willing listener, we soon discover that the other person needs and wants to share their own struggles with us. This mutual sharing and intimacy is often very helpful for we discover that we are being affirmed when we allow ourselves to be vulnerable and honest. The openness and caring that we find in such a partner will further our personal growth and development. A patient consulting an effective therapist may also receive the same kind of affirmation and support. Those of us who are willing to share ourselves and our struggles are creating and furthering deep intimacy with others. The individuals who are and remain strong and silent will frequently keep others at a distance, thereby creating and maintaining superficial and often empty relationships.

I hope to provide in this book some basic tools and ideas that can be used for self-exploration. To recognize that we all both change and do not change, and that we rarely have understood or willfully directed these changes is both a startling and, I am sure, unsettling insight. However, once one realizes that personal changes have often occurred without deliberation, then one can also acknowledge that it is possible to intentionally create desired changes in a more straightforward and productive manner.

We are all works in progress and, hopefully, will own the truth that we are the artists who can change the collage that exists at this moment. We are more than a canvas for we recognize that we have the capacity to be powerful agents of personal change. However, in order to make good changes in the collage, it will be very helpful first to study the substance of that collage.

Experiencing

I feel extraordinarily wonderful when I am swimming in a fairly calm Atlantic ocean with water temperature in the 70s. At those moments a broad smile appears on my face, I am deeply in tune with nature and I know that I am fully experiencing the awesome wonder of being alive. It seems impossible to imagine that my mind and body could feel any more energized or more at peace than when I am so immersed in that particular experience. Yes, I am saying that I love swimming, but that phrase does such a weak job of conveying what this type of swimming means to me. How and what I am feeling when I am in the ocean is my own special personal experience — my own unique reality. Furthermore, how I feel when I am swimming in salt water is very different from how I feel when I am swimming in a pool or lake. The range of feelings I have when in I am in the water is likely to be very different from what other people feel when they are swimming. I am well aware that a large number of people have no interest in swimming. Also, I regularly see that many people can and will spend a day at the beach and never go into the water. Even though I understand that they prefer to sun bathe rather than to bathe in the water, a part of me finds their behavior incomprehensible. For me, I only enjoy the heat of the sun if I can quickly cool off in the water. Getting hot without getting cool would be intolerable. When I am having such a wonderful experience, it seems foreign to me that another person would find that same experience undesirable.

One January when I was vacationing in Florida, I noticed that no one was swimming in the ocean. I dipped my feet in the water and found the temperature warm and comfortable, but I was unwilling to venture farther until I could determine why no one else was in the water. The hotel desk clerk told me that the water temperature, in the low 70s, was considered too cold by the natives who, therefore, would not go swimming. I, a north-easterner, was astounded because rarely does the temperature at our local shores ever reach into the high 70s. What I consider ideal swimming temperatures is what southerners consider too cold.

I see that my experiences when swimming are very much my own feelings and, therefore, are likely to be different from the ways that other people feel. My ongoing experiences are not necessarily hidden, but at every moment I am experiencing, and only rarely am I able to describe my experiences of the moment to another human being. I am continually experiencing and, most importantly, these experiences are very personal. I wish it were true that other people had the same experiences that

I do. I would feel validated if others saw and felt in the same ways that I do, but I really doubt that can be true. I am living in my own skin, having my own experiences and no one else fully knows what these experiences are. Certainly, I often try to share my experiences. I gladly talk with others and listen, and often we hope that we have shared perceptions and experiences.

In order to communicate what I am feeling to other people I must use words, but all words are one step removed from the experience itself. Despite the fact that people will use identical words in their communications, these words often conjure up different images and feelings for each person. Words do have basic and universal meaning when they are defined simply and used in a narrow sense; but we humans rarely experience words in a narrow sense as we give them a host of associative meanings. For example, consider all the extended meanings we give to the word "liberal." You can find ten different meanings for the word in the dictionary, but even more importantly, there are different emotional connotations given to the word. For some people liberal is broad-minded and positive, implying an acceptance of diversity. For others, liberal means weak-minded, free-spending and unrealistic.

Many years ago I found a classic example of this diametric difference in the associative meanings given to words when I was preparing lecture notes for a social psychology class. I was preparing to discuss the authoritarian personality, which is a character type typically described as "rigid, using denial, being power-oriented but exploitatively dependent with a sexual partner, and who gravitates toward a political philosophy which preaches strength and demeans weakness." (Adorno, T.W., Frenkel-Brunswik, E., Levinson, D.J., & Sanford, R.N., 1950). This American-based understanding of the authoritarian personality was the result of a large scale research project conducted after World War II. This study was initiated due to a nationwide concern over whether fascism could become popular in the United States. The research study began as an attempt to understand people who held anti-Semitic views, but it was soon recognized that anti-Semitic sentiments were part of a larger character structure which then became described as the "authoritarian personality."

Some 15 years earlier a German Nazi supporter reported upon what he called the J type of personality, who has characteristics similar to the authoritarian personality. However, the J type person was described as making clear and unambiguous perceptual judgments, and as being tough and masculine. Also, the J type person was described as knowing that human behavior is fixed by blood, soil and national tradition and being of north German ancestry. What is important to notice here is that the same characteristics are described as flaws and deficiencies in the authoritarian personality and are simultaneously glorified in the Nazi depiction of the Aryan character.

It becomes apparent that the same behaviors can be described as very positive by one person and as very negative by another. What we Americans called rigidity, the fascists labeled as clear and firm. What we see as exploitive behavior, the fascists considered to be masculine. Very frequently behaviors are interpreted from different value positions so that any two individuals can view the same behavior patterns and give them radically different meanings and interpretations. Such basic differences in perception makes it extraordinarily difficult for us to be able to set aside our own viewpoint and understand the experiences of another without the taint of our own value judgments.

On an even more basic level, the words that we use have a host of individual associated meanings beyond their simple dictionary definitions. Therefore, when we think of or use a particular word, a chain of personal associations has begun. We hold many of these associated meanings in common with other people; but it is highly unlikely, perhaps impossible, for all of us to have the same chain of meanings to each word. For example, consider the word *feminine* which means female, or attractive, or weak or powerful, depending upon the mind set of the listener. Associative meanings are activated even when we do not use these words aloud for we think in words as well as in images. Still, words are the one important and primary way in which we make sense of our experiences.

An example can make this point much clearer. Let us regard the term *cold.* When we use the word *cold* to signify body temperature we still cannot know what *cold* really feels like to another person. For me *cold* conjures up the kind of winter weather where my toes feel like they cannot move or the tips of my fingers feel numb. *Cold* for other people describes a wind that cuts through one's sinuses like a knife. Such a person can be *cold* in 75 degree weather if the wind is blowing. I never find 75 degree weather *cold* because I find warm breezes refreshing. If the temperature were to drop to 25 degrees with a heavy wind, then certainly I would be *cold.* Again, *cold* holds different connotations for different people even when it is used to describe physical temperature and not a personality characteristic.

These few example demonstrate that we all have our own ways of experiencing the world, and each of our own experiences is different from what others are experiencing. Not only are we likely to experience the same events differently but these experiences will continue to vary over time. We all are processes of experiencing that extend over time. We all are continually experiencing beings whose experiences are ongoing and basically private. Furthermore, because we are all continually engaged in our own experiencing, most of our personal experiences will never be shared with another living soul.

Appearances can also be kept private by choice. Some of my own fantasies need to remain only my own because I am well aware that at times I will have weird, illogical and bizarre thoughts. I am sure that all of us, at times, suffer from such uncomfortable and unacceptable images. Most of us recognize that these fantasies are basically alien to who and to what we are. Therefore, we do not want to give these fantasies any legitimacy by speaking of them in public. We want to hide these parts both from others and from ourselves as well. Instead we choose to communicate those ideas that we want others to hear and to understand. We also share our meaningful experiences with those other people whom we believe will be most receptive to us and to our ideas. We all need and want to be understood and validated by other people, and the only way to gain such validation is by sharing our own thoughts and feelings through communication.

To better understand oneself as an experiencing process it is necessary to engage in careful self-study. Because no one else can fully know the uniqueness of our own experiences, we each have to become our basic source of evaluation. When we study ourselves as experiential processes, we see that we exist in our own personal experiences which are both ongoing and changing processes. Although others may assume they know what our experiences are, our experiences cannot be seen by others because they are fundamentally private and can only partly be shared and understood through communication.

I use the word experience to describe whatever we know is going on within us. Other words convey what people know about themselves, the most frequently used being consciousness. Experience and consciousness basically mean the same thing but again they have different connotations. For me the word consciousness is an intellectual and objective description of a person's internal process. In contrast, the word experience seems to convey the actual feelings one has. There are other words which are synonyms yet one of the words seems to describe the condition in more intellectual terms while the other word better expresses the feelings. The two specific words I am referring to are anxiety, the more intellectual description; and dread, which immediately and more fully conveys the awful pit felt in one's stomach. However, each of us has our own personal association to words so that the word anxiety can readily conjure up feelings for one particular person even though it does not effectively describe a feeling state for a different person. It is very important that we choose our words carefully and also that we attempt to most fully understand what the other person means when they use particular terms.

At this point, I need to remind you, my readers, that a part of me remains the university professor. Accordingly, when I discuss specific ideas I must credit the original authors of these concepts by providing you with references. In those short sections (one of which immediately follows) you may feel as if you are sitting in a classroom. However, I believe these ideas are very important and warrant both references and discussion.

Because the terms experience and consciousness are synonyms, some earlier writings which describe the nature of consciousness provide important insights into understanding ourselves as experiential processes. William James (1890), who wrote the first American psychology book, devoted one chapter to a description of consciousness, a description that remains relevant and very meaningful today. James said that once we admit that consciousness of some sort goes on within us, we will be able to see that consciousness has four basic characteristics. First, one must recognize that every state of consciousness is part of a personal consciousness. In other words, we only know our own consciousness and we cannot know the abstract condition called consciousness.

I personally know what I am conscious of, and all the consciousness that I possess is my own special and unique experience of things. When I try to understand the consciousness of someone else, I can only know it through the filter of my own consciousness. In fact, everything that I do know is known through myself as a process of consciousness.

James' second characteristic of each personal consciousness is that it is always changing. We experience something different at each moment in time for our experiences are continually in flux. James used the phrase "stream of consciousness" to describe the continuing changes or movement of our experiencing. Something is always happening in our consciousness. We do not keep the same image or fixate upon the same thought. Rather, our mind moves in leaps and bounds. When we study what is happening in our consciousness, we can see that our consciousness functions as if it were a motion picture, because the images or thoughts that are present keep changing.

We humans are continually bombarded by both internal and external experiences. Some of what is happening outside of us is registered by our senses, so that we see, hear, taste, feel and touch. Hosts of external stimuli are always impinging upon us but we only directly attend to a few of these factors. Not only are we being bombarded by these external events but at the same time numbers of internal events are also regularly occurring. These internal events have been given different names such as thoughts, dreams, fantasies and emotions. In our stream of consciousness there are veritable parades of both internal and external processes. To believe that we ourselves, or our consciousness, could remain the same in the face of this continuing stimulation is not logical according to James. The continuing internal and external bombardment produces a continuing change in the content of our consciousness.

James describes the third characteristic of consciousness as being sensibly continuous. Even though our consciousness moves from place to place and from topic to topic, at times even at lightening speed, these rapid changes in content still feel perfectly natural to us. We are rarely disarmed or disoriented at the quick flow of our thoughts or experiences. Whatever goes on in our mind seems to make sense to us. We may move from unrelated topic to unrelated topic, from feeling to thinking in a totally haphazard fashion, and these changes in the content of our consciousness do not bother us. James says there is a mechanism in consciousness that allows us to make these rapid changes as the stream of consciousness can operate at two different speeds. The substantive nature of consciousness is the place where our consciousness stays or rests. When our attention remains focused upon any particular topic, we are using the operation of the substantive nature of consciousness. We also have mechanisms in our consciousness that enable it to move or shift from topic to topic which he calls the transitions of consciousness. Words like *if, and, but* and *however* are some of the transitional words that allow our consciousness to move quickly from topic to topic. These mechanisms function as the glue that enables us to connect unrelated topics. As a result, we feel basically quite comfortable no matter in what direction our mind wanders.

The fourth characteristic of our consciousness is that it always knows where it is going. James said that consciousness has a fringe, or a sense of direction. For example, if we were to start a sentence in a foreign language we would continue to speak in that language. Our mind or our consciousness appears to know where it is going for we are rarely, if ever, disoriented by our thoughts. In other words, we utter one sentence after another, knowing that the sentences all make sense; but we do not deliberately plan our sentences before we utter them. As it actually happens, words simply tumble out of our mouths. They are indeed our words and they feel right after we have uttered them, but we rarely, if ever, know specifically exactly what we are about to say before we actually say it. James described this condition by saying that consciousness is more interested in some things than it is in others and it is constantly choosing all of the time what to focus on and where to go.

The last of James' remarkable insights about consciousness is one most people find quite unsettling. We can readily accept the idea that our consciousness is personal, that it expresses our own world and our experiences. We would have no real difficulty in acknowledging that our consciousness is ever-changing, for we know that to be true. That our experiences and thoughts seem quite sensible to us is, of course, reassuring because we like to believe that we are indeed rational creatures. What makes us pause and feel disoriented is James' description of how consciousness moves.

James points out that our stream of consciousness is not under our own direct or willful control. Rather, we are pulled along by our stream of consciousness. We do not willfully or purposly direct the stream of our consciousness. It is only very rarely that we are able to focus our mind upon a particular topic. The overwhelming majority of the time we do not choose what to experience for our experiencing immediately happens without the use of our deliberate will power. Even when there are times that we concentrate our attention on a particular topic, we soon discover that "our mind wanders" and that such wandering is, in fact, the basic and correct description of the nature of our stream of consciousness.

We are regularly and simply conscious, and what is occurring in our consciousness is not the result of our deliberate thought or will power. Instead, we are best described as *in* the process of experiencing and our experiencing is always instantaneous. We do not choose whether to experience or not to experience because our experiencing is ongoing. We are not in control of our experiences. Rather, what we are experiencing is what pulls us in certain directions. Once a person becomes willing to concede that James' insights into consciousness are correct, then it becomes both possible and, indeed, necessary to change the ways in which one sees oneself.

The analogy I often used in my classes to describe our relationship with our consciousness was to have the students picture themselves as driving a mule cart, for that image conveys both the correct and incorrect ways one can conceptualize consciousness. When asked about themselves and their consciousness, most students would say that they were proceeding through life as if they were the driver of the mule cart. In other words, they usually believed they controlled the direction of their consciousness. However, James' description of consciousness portrays a very different truth. His implication is that we are living and experiencing our lives as if we were the mule rather than if we were the driver. The mule appears to be the better representation of consciousness because mules go where they want to go and only rarely follow the driver's directions. We all would prefer to believe that we direct our consciousness just as we would much prefer to see ourselves as the driver who tells the mule where to go.

Actually, the better explanation is that we are both the mule and the driver of the cart. Occasionally we do change the direction of our consciousness by making ourselves focus our attention and our consciousness. However, it is always the mule who moves the cart, irrespective of the driver's attempts to steer. Most of us have not recognized that the mule or, more importantly, our consciousness functions as an independent but central part of ourselves.

That mule is the better representation of our consciousness or our experience. Whenever we tell ourselves that we are the driver of the mule cart, we are implicitly asserting that we are the intellectual thinker, problem solver or guide who directs our voyage in life. However, we are not simply able to use our will to regularly steer our consciousness nor are we able to make the mule move in the direction or at the pace we want. The mule is a representation of ourselves and we need to expand the ways we understand ourselves acknowledging that our experiences are neither directed nor guided but that they simply happen. That immediate ongoing experiencing is truly the central part of how we lead our lives. Until we embrace this truth, we restrict our self-image and our understanding of ourselves.

It is difficult to abandon the belief that we are in control of our minds and our actions. To believe that our "mind" is directing us without knowing how or why can leave us feeling quite lost. Accordingly, we have created "explanations" that give us the illusion that we are really in control of what is going on. The simplest such explanation used is expressed in the statement that whatever occurs in our minds is a consequence of our thinking. We easily turn to such an explanation because, beginning early in life, we all were told that we can and do think, and we want to believe that indeed our thinking is what is producing the images that flood our consciousness.

In the 17th century René Descartes used the power of logic and reason to prove his existence. He said *I think, therefore, I am.* This particular formulation continues to have a profound effect upon much of Western civilization, for many of us do agree that Descartes was indeed correct. Descartes essentially proclaimed that reason (or thinking) was the central and most important human characteristic. It was only through the use of reason that one could know anything. Indeed, following Descartes' logic, one could not even be sure of personal existence without the use of deductive reasoning.

By elevating reason and thinking to the highest status in the human being, Descartes led us to place greatest value on our rational capacity. This reverence for thinking is still endorsed and used throughout all levels of education. Most of us have learned to believe that our behaviors can be understood as a consequence of our thinking. If we engage in *bad behavior,* it is because we have not thought. To be certain about something, we are supposed to think long and hard about it. Many of us believe that we humans are the highest form of life because we alone can use reason whereas other animals cannot use logic and reason to control their lives.

Thinking and reason are wonderful tools we have at our disposal. Many of us, when in the throes of decision-making, devise lists of pros and cons in order to help reach a resolution and to make the best possible choice. In such instances one typically writes all the advantages and disadvantages of one choice and compares this list with the advantages and disadvantages of the other choice. When we see which option offers the greater advantages (and if we are fundamentally rational), we will select the better option. However, in truth, it is rare that such list making really leads us to make our final decision.

Instead, we may be engaged in a minor form of self-deception. Most of us usually favor one alternative even without admitting it to ourselves. We may find that even though the list favors one alternative, we still do not feel quite right about following that choice. Or we may ask a friend for an opinion but only accept a suggestion if it follows our own leaning. At other times we find ourselves in the midst of carrying out what we can call alternative A. If asked why alternative A, we would most likely say that we must have thought that A was the better alternative. However, in most instances we do not really know what, if anything, we actually thought. Instead we find ourselves acting as if we had already made a deliberate choice when that was not the case at all.

Indeed, the more accurate description is that often we behave without having directly engaged in rational thinking. We open the refrigerator door and look for food, but we did not specifically ask ourselves if we want to eat or not. This immediacy of action is similar to the mechanism of our speech, for whenever we speak, the words seemingly just spill out of our mouths and these words are rarely planned. After we speak, if we take the time to evaluate what we have just said, usually we recognize that what we have said has made good sense. If someone quizzed us further and asked us to provide a better explanation for our words, most of us would probably state that we said whatever it was that we had meant to say, or that our speech reflected our intentions. However, often we did not consciously or specifically know exactly what we were going to say before we said it.

We are all moving, speaking and acting without having first deliberately and rationally planned our thoughts and actions. If asked to explain why we moved, spoke or acted in a particular way, we could consider the question and most likely then be able provide a logical explanation. But we did not have that answer at our fingertips at the moment we started to engage in the behavior. Rather, we simply and immediately behaved just as we simply and immediately breathed. We typically breathe without thinking and, in fact, when we start to think about our breathing, we have trouble because the breathing then becomes labored. Our actions, our speech and most of our behavior appears to simply happen, but we all know that it is not random or haphazard. Rather, whatever we are doing we must have intended to do because when we do it (speak, move or behave), these actions and experiences feel right to us. Therefore, in some manner we must indeed know what we wish to be doing and we simply proceed to do it. Such directed action can be described as a form of "intentionality" which is quite different from what we call "rational thinking."

We therefore *know* what to say, where to go, how to do things and all of this knowing is immediate and typically present at every moment. Such knowing is basic to all of us. It is a knowing without thinking. This form of knowing has been labeled by existential writers as *prereflective consciousness*. It is very different from knowing by the use of thinking which is called *reflective consciousness*.

Each of us has been taught, either directly or implicitly, that reflective consciousness is the highest form of knowing. We have been taught that we can make our best choices by relying upon our reflective consciousness. However, we spend most of our lives functioning in the realm of prereflective consciousness. We all immediately *know* and are aware in each moment, but most of us would prefer to say that the reason we know in the moment is because we have thought about what is going on. We need to use the explanation that we have engaged in thinking in order to feel reassured and to believe that we are, in fact, rational creatures. However, we do know when we are actually functioning as reflective consciousness, i.e., when we are actually thinking; and the rest of the time we must admit that we are not actually thinking but are functioning through the mode of prereflective consciousness.

We do not know that we have actually thought or planned what is in our mind at any given moment. All we really can know is what is actually happening now. We can acknowledge that we are indeed experiencing something at this particular moment. To say that our thinking has produced our experiences is to make a hypothesis that does not really explain anything. We very well know at what times we are actually thinking. We know what it feels like to deliberate and ponder over things. Again, we all know what it is like to be functioning as reflective consciousness.

To believe that our thoughts produce our experiences reiterates the belief that we, or a part of ourselves, is driving the mule cart. But we have no way of really knowing that is the case. Sigmund Freud created his own imaginary *driver* when he developed the idea of the unconscious ego. He essentially said that our unconscious ego knows what is happening at all times and that the unconscious ego is in control of our consciousness. In other words, he created an intangible concept, the ego, as a supposed explanation of the existence of thinking. However, the idea of the ego only provides us with a comfortable illusion, for now we *supposedly* understand why things happen. A fictional concept that we can never see nor measure cannot be a sufficient explanation for our thinking.

The simpler truth, which is quite difficult and perhaps painful for all of us to accept, is that we are continually experiencing new things and we do not know why these experiences happen. In fact we do not decide what it is we will or will not experience. Our experiencing is the source of whatever happens and it is first and foremost what makes us ourselves. We need to embrace the importance of our experiencing as a basic way of describing our own personal identity.

An even better way of following and being able to understand this viewpoint is that you know what it is to be an experiencing process because you live it. Other people, especially psychologists or psychiatrists, may see and even define you, the reader, as a creature who behaves or who thinks. That is certainly one way of describing you. However, if they study or know you only as a behaving or thinking creature they will not capture who the essential *you* is. They will not know that you live as an experiencing creature and that those experiences are the crucial and central parts of who you are.

Redefining yourself as an experiencing process can be disorienting as well as very exciting. Actually it can and will be both things at different moments. Perhaps it would be best if you, the reader, take the time to "think" about what I have said and see if it makes good sense. You can effectively use reflective consciousness to enhance your prereflective consciousness. In other words, we can find great value in being both the mule and the driver. Thinking, or reflective consciousness, can make the actions of our prereflective consciousness appear to have been well thought out or even brilliant.

Once we admit that we primarily function as prereflective consciousness then we must admit that other people also understand their world through their prereflective consciousness. As we listen to and attempt to understand others, we basically will be using the knowing of our prereflective consciousness. In the immediacy of the moment we will understand and make sense of what others are doing and saying, without taking time to think about their actions. At other times we will think about the other person's actions and attempt to understand them by drawing upon the problem solving ability of our reflective consciousness.

To function well in the world we must first be able to understand others before we can communicate effectively with them. Most of us attend to what others say or do and use this information as basic cues for understanding. In that regard, the lay person uses the same basic principles as does the professional psychologist in making attempts to understand people. We all in some way study and interpret the meaning of other people's behavior. Certainly, what individuals do may tell us important things about them. However, a person's actions do not directly tell us the actual experiencing. Oftentimes there is logical consistency between a person's experience and the person's behavior. At other times, one's personal experiences are quite different from one's actions; this is especially true when the intent is to deceive the other person. In some such instances people with a deceptive agenda may act in a warm and friendly manner even though their feelings are hostile.

However, our outward behavior and our personal ongoing experiencing may be quite different, even when we are not trying to be deceptive. For example, often when one is driving a car, the driving is done almost automatically but with one's mind someplace else. At such times, one can have driven from a store to home seemingly without directly attending to driving, because of engagement in some form of thinking or problem solving.

These two simple examples point out that any attempt to understand another person simply by attending to the outward behavior will be deficient. It is necessary to try as much as possible to understand others as being processes of ongoing experiencing, which means an attempt to look inside the person instead of only looking at outside behavior.

Different methods and techniques can be used to try to understand the experiences of others. One useful strategy is to try to feel what others feel by imagining ourselves as being in their shoes. We can listen carefully to what they are saying and through trial, error and discussion, we can better hear how and what they are experiencing. These strategies for understanding others have been labeled by psychologists as phenomenological methods. In a lay person's terms, such actions are described as empathic. For example, when I watch a football game I often find myself moving my foot at the same time that a place kicker is trying to make a field goal. My moving foot is an expression of my felt empathy. There have also been occasions when in conducting psychotherapy I discovered that tears filled my eyes, another manifestation of my empathy as I was experiencing the pain of another person. When I used my reflective consciousness to understand my tears, I saw that a strange phenomenon had taken place. The tears in my eyes were usually a manifestation of the pain that was somewhere in the client, but the client was not feeling that pain in the moment. I had managed to have the experience that these clients would not allow for themselves at least in that moment.

Even when we become adept at understanding another person's experience at the moment, the moment always changes and the person is also changing. Our understanding then immediately becomes past history and is not necessarily relevant for the next moment. Understanding the other's experience is extremely difficult; therefore, both professionals and laymen often abandon any attempt to do so. Unfortunately, many psychologists have tried to circumvent this difficulty by stating that people's experiences do not need to be studied. However, because we are so centrally experiencing creatures, to circumvent the study of experience is to commit a major error.

As a person, and as a psychologist, I know that my experiences are who I essentially am. The part of me that was trained to be a scientist knows how difficult or even impossible it is to study the experiences of another person. Nonetheless, I continue to try to understand people as experiencing processes because I know that is what I am and that is what each person is as well.

There is a particular part of me other people can and do know. That is a "me" that exists in the eyes of the other. Each other person *knows* a different me. That part contains my past behaviors that were seen, noticed and remembered by others. However, the "me" that others see is different from the "me" of my own personal experiences which is the most important "me" to myself. If others want to know who I am, they must attempt to know this personally experiencing "me."

In many different situations we focus on understanding the experiences of others. Many of us enjoy reading novels because these books do an excellent job of describing what other people are feeling. One of the most special aspects of being in the throes of a beginning love affair is that we are able to share our deepest experiences. In so doing we feel deeply understood, perhaps even for the first time, which enhances the feelings of true intimacy. Of course, in effective psychotherapy the therapist must also focus upon understanding and validating the experiences of the client.

The formal educational process pays little attention to what a person experiences or how information is processed. It has become far too important for many educators to focus upon demanding that the student simply acquire "necessary" information and data. How that information or data is experienced, and how it coexists with the other information that a person has already acquired, is rarely given particular attention. We are much more than repositories of information. It is how we experience things and the importance we give to these particular experiences that conveys who we most essentially are.

For better self-understanding it becomes very useful to accept a new definition of oneself as a *process of experiencing*. This *process of experiencing* functions both as a prereflective consciousness as well as a reflective consciousness. We need to accept the truth that other people can and must be seen in this same new way that we define ourselves. We can use our reflective consciousness to study the ways in which we experience things and to better understand others. In addition, this new definition of self opens us to gaining new insights about how to function more effectively in our experiential world.

We are Verbs

As we come to accept ourselves as experiencing creatures, we need to distinguish between what we experience and how we experience it. For example, sometimes we are hungry and sometimes we are HUNGRY! We can have very intense feelings at some times and be basically unresponsive at other times. We will misunderstand ourselves in a most basic way if we only attend to *what* we are feeling without attending to *how* we are feeling it.

Medard Boss (1963) believed it was crucial to study how we experience things at any given moment. He used the term *pitch* to convey how *sharp* or how *flat* people were in attending to and encountering their world. Boss recognized that at times we are very open; we can hear and listen and understand. At other times we are primarily shut off and inattentive to what transpires around us. Furthermore, we can create such openness or perpetuate closed-ness in our experience. For example, when we meet a friend our mood often elevates – we smile and listen carefully and convey our good feelings in a number of verbal and nonverbal ways. On the other hand, when we are doing something that we do not like, our mood sinks and we are likely to become gruff, stand-offish and minimally responsive. We can also shift from closed-ness to openness instantaneously and seemingly without even knowing why these changes take place.

Rapid shifts in both how and what we experience are commonplace. On the other hand we all often experience the same things, over and over again. Therefore, we are both changing processes as well as non-changing processes, and we need to better understand why both stability and change are necessary.

Because we live in a social world, we continually receive feedback from other people about who we are and what we are. Furthermore, we have learned it is necessary to regularly present and categorize ourselves in particular ways in order to be effective with others. Hardly a week goes by where we are not required to fill out various forms asking us to catalogue ourselves through demographic or sociological data such as age, sex, occupation, social security number or credit card data. We are so accustomed to thinking about ourselves and others in these sociological terms that often, upon meeting strangers, we frequently ask their occupation. In some communities people are catalogued based simply upon the street on which they live.

When we use such categorizations either to approach or avoid others, we do not recognize the other person as an experiencing process. Instead we relegate them to a particular status based upon their occupation. Unfortunately, far too many people are rejected simply because they do not have the *right* kind of job, position or social status. Many women have often been dismissed as being in some way deficient because they do not hold a job outside of the home. It may occasionally be helpful to have some sociological data, such as whether one was raised by a single parent, in order not to make a social gaffe; but such information does not convey the basic essence of the person. Knowing how a person spends a specific number of hours per week does not efficiently communicate the passion or perhaps lack of commitment for that occupation. Specific activities such as work can be a central and vital part of one's own experiential world, but it may be secondary or unimportant compared to the other activities in another person's life.

We can far too easily fall into such overgeneralized thinking if we do not pay enough careful attention. The first time I specifically realized that I had been using such stereotyped thinking was in early graduate training. I had to obtain a social history from a woman who had brought her daughter to the psychological clinic for assistance. One of the routine questions was whether the mother had breast-fed or bottle-fed her child. This particular woman, who appeared rather cold and rejecting, stated that she had breast-fed. I was startled by her statement and soon realized that as a somewhat naive young man, I had engaged in stereotypic thinking, believing that a woman would breast-feed her child as a special way of expressing her warmth. As this woman described breast vs bottle feeding she said that she "couldn't be bothered with all the fuss of sterilizing bottles but instead, one - two - three, you put the baby to your breast and it will be over quickly."

That interview provided a very important lesson by demonstrating that *how* we do things can be even more important than *what* we do. For example, bottle feeding a baby can be an especially warm, loving process, and breast-feeding can be conducted in a very cold manner. A mundane task such as sweeping a floor can be a humdrum, boring task which is viewed as an unwanted intrusion on one's time. On the other hand, some custodians will take pride in how clean they have made the workplace.

Demographic data such as sex, age and occupation may provide information about the world of objective reality, but it does not necessarily correspond to what the person is experiencing. To fill out a questionnaire and specify that you are either male or female seems to be asserting a simple biological fact. However, some people who have the outward biological characteristics of one sex do not consider themselves to be of that sex and may undergo surgery to change what others consider an immutable truth. While it is most common for people to accept their outer biology as their inner biology, i.e., males are male and females are female, there is still much controversy over what it means to be a woman or a man. Does calling oneself female or male really signify something beyond the possession of specific sexual organs? For many people being male or female certainly implies a host of different characteristics that go far beyond whether or not one possesses a Y chromosome.

In our society it remains quite common to socialize boys and girls differently. Bestowing toy guns on boys and giving dolls to girls is one form of sexual stereotyping that can begin early in life and which many parents do without much thought. Often when parents decide not to give their sons toy guns, swords or tanks, they do so because of their belief in nonviolence rather than in opposition to sexual stereotyping. Irrespective of particular parental expectations it is extraordinarily difficult to find popular entertainment that does not routinely depict males as engaged in aggressive behavior. In contrast, movies with the slang designation of *chick flicks* are supposed to stress the importance of caring in relationships.

The long-standing sexual stereotyping in our society causes many boys to believe they must prove they are *real men*. To demonstrate maleness means to exhibit aggression and power as well as dominance over others. Obviously, individuals who think in this manner consider maleness to signify something quite beyond simple biology. Their definition of masculinity reflects their psychology much more than it expresses their biology. Such thinking is far too institutionalized in our culture despite much of the progress made toward equality between the sexes. All too often I still encounter male psychotherapy clients who wonder if they could be gay simply because they are not interested in sports or aggressive behavior.

Because aggression has so commonly been labeled as a male characteristic, when females become aggressive or even assertive, they run the risk of being labeled as *castrating females*. By creating such a phrase, our society has implied that a man's masculinity can indeed be taken away by a woman. The female can be accused of being castrating when she does not assume a deferential role with a man. If the male does not assume a dominating or superior position with a woman, he can accuse himself of having lost his masculinity.

Before the feminist movement, the term *feminine* did not have the connotation of power, as being feminine implied taking a subordinate position to a male. For that reason, there is no phrase in our language that implies that a male can take away a female's femininity. Unfortunately, the reason that the woman could always retain her psychological femininity was that femininity has been historically equated with inferiority. When a woman asserts her power, she is often accused of *growing balls*. These observations, that in western society masculinity has been equated with superiority and femininity with inferiority, were very clearly stated by Alfred Adler (1968). His understanding of the problematic equation of masculinity with power and femininity with powerlessness is still quite relevant in today's world and most certainly appears to be rampant in many third world countries.

Our society would be much healthier if we continued to reduce and finally eliminate sexual stereotyping. In the meantime, the male who does not show an interest in aggression or in sports remains at risk of being labeled as unmanly by his peers. The high-achieving female is liable to be criticized for not acting as a woman. If these terms, male and female, are considered to be transient states that can be gained or lost through specific behavior patterns, then we must re-examine the validity of the concept of objective truths. In fact, most of the other simple and objective truths which are usually considered non-controversial and unalterable are, indeed, impermanent and changeable. Passive people can change their outlook and become active. Smart people do act dumb in some situations and dumb people act smart in other situations. Because we all can and do change, we must be careful in accepting objective descriptions as conveying the real truths of who and what we are.

Objective facts, or the items that one checks off on a questionnaire such as age, sex, interests etc., are not necessarily experienced as being subjective or experienced truths. Often when we fill out questionnaires we do so automatically and without question. People who state *I am 19 years of age* can have many different perceptions of what it means to be 19. Some people see 19 as a time of total freedom, others may see it as a time where they must prove themselves, others as standing on the cusp of adulthood, etc. For some, 19 is not being old enough, while for others 19 is the perfect age. An objective fact does not stand by itself for it has different connotations for different people. Consequently, what is true in the eyes of others is not necessarily what is true for oneself. We cannot assume that we all give the same meanings to objective facts.

For example, at the moment I began writing this text, I was in my 60s. The age is an objective fact, but it does not at all convey what I am experiencing. I often feel shocked when I acknowledge my chronological age because I do not feel the way I think I *should* feel. To be quite honest, I really do not know what one is supposed to feel like when they are in their seventh decade. I suppose when I was much younger and paid scant attention to my elders, I believed that a person who had logged that many years must feel incredibly old. Certainly, there are times when I do feel quite old, but there are many more times when I feel very young. Most of the time my age does not enter into my experience of anything. Instead of focusing upon my age, I simply experience whatever is going on at the moment, rarely connecting it with my chronological age. Because years have passed since I began this writing, I now view age 62 as a past age of mine, which does not seem much different from when I was 57. However, if I pondered the differences between those ages I would remember important life events that occurred over that time period. I would be able to catalogue how I, myself, had changed in both minor and major ways over those years. When we reflect over our past, we may make better sense of the significance of our chronological age. However, when we focus upon living in the here and the now, age rarely becomes an important issue. Nonetheless, at times I am shocked at the looks of the person I see in the mirror, for he is much older than I am!

The major reason for discussing chronological age is to demonstrate that the only important meaning age has is what the person gives to it. If I label myself as old and have a host of negative associative connotations toward being old, I will no doubt become depressed. Because I am typically much more upbeat, I am more likely to associate being *old* with being experienced and wise rather than "over the hill." When holding discussions in my existential psychology course, I often responded to some comments by saying that I was younger than all of the students there. I meant that I viewed these students as very staid and stuffy, and I felt more adventuresome about the prospects of living than they did.

One way to better understand the difference between experienced reality and objective reality is to ask yourself "when and where am I a child? Am I a daughter or a son when I am in school or when I am with a lover?" According to questionnaire data, one is always an offspring, but the fact that we have parents rarely directly affects our behavior in specific situations. We may be considerate because we learned that from parents, but how we respond in the moment in particular situations is much more a consequence of how we see that moment. It would be worrisome if you felt like your parent's child when in the company of your lover.

Can an offspring fully disown a parent and no longer be the child of one's biological parents? Being a daughter or son is neither a constant experiential condition nor is it a simple or universal biological fact. One can be a biological son and never acknowledge that one's biological parent is, in fact, one's real parent. One can be a son to adopted parents and even be a son to someone where no formal adoption has taken place. One can even be a son to one parent and not a son to the other parent.

These observations point out how difficult it is to effectively define what it means to be a daughter or a son. Does it mean a set of obligations and duties or privileges? Does it mean nothing in particular? Because categorical terms have a host of different associated meanings, we do not have simple truths which can be meaningful guideposts for living. Instead, we need to recognize that we are each experiencing and defining our world and through this process we are creating our own personal truths.

All of us have had our own experiences of what it is to be a particular sex and age, and of an ethnic group and particular occupation. These are our past experiences. As such, they cannot be changed. What I was and how I was in the past can also be classified objectively, just as I can now be classified as of a particular age, sex and occupation today. It is also possible that I can experience or think of myself as being a member of these different categories and, therefore, not open to change. What I was can, therefore, be categorized as the part of me that is a noun—the unchangeable past.

However, all people are works in progress which means that we each live in our own private experiential worlds and can always continue to grow and to develop. Perhaps the best English word to describe this facet of the human condition is that we are all *becoming*. Emerging and changing are both *ing* words and *ing* words are verbs. In fact, we all are verbs. Jean Paul Sartre (1956) put it beautifully when he said that we are verbs who are continually trying to become nouns. In his terminology we are *being for onself* (verbs) who are trying to become *being in itself* (nouns).

Sartre further pointed out that it is quite uncomfortable for us to accept the truth that we are verbs (or capable of change). We lose our illusions of having a sense of stability or permanence if we cannot trust that we will be the same tomorrow as we are today. We want to see ourselves as having several fixed characteristics such as I am an athlete, mother, scholar or child, as these characteristics provide us with an anchor for our dealings in the world. We feel some assurance by viewing ourselves as having certain permanent characteristics. However, Sartre tells us that such is not the truth. Our belief, that we have a static self, can become our personal experienced truth only at a particular moment and only when we accept this belief as the truth. It is not a permanent truth because, as works in progress, we naturally continue to change. Therefore, we can alter any or all of the characterizations of ourselves that we may have believed at a particular moment.

Even though we cannot change what has happened in our past, we can change the meanings that we give to our past experiences. When we consider our past at the current moment, we can understand our earlier behaviors in a different light. Such new understanding of our past, or the achievement of insight, is one of the prime benefits that people can gain from personal psychotherapy.

To recognize that we are works in progress and to know that we can and do change are vital insights for powerful healthy living. At each particular moment we can become free of what has defined us in the past because we are, in fact, verbs. In grammar, verbs express action and existence. When we reject the fact that we can function as verbs, we continue to see ourselves as nouns, fixed and unchangeable entities, and hence be unable to alter our lives. We need to acknowledge that we have been nouns in the sense that we have a past that cannot be changed. However, it is much more important in the immediate moment to recognize that we are verbs who can act in ways totally independent of our past histories. We may have acted meekly for a number of years and then suddenly and immediately become bold and forceful. It is that capacity to step outside of the familiar and to boldly initiate change that is one of the most lovable of human qualities. Such behavior clearly affirms the truth that we are verbs.

I firmly believe that the way we can feel most fully alive is by embracing the truth that we are verbs. When we are no longer alive, we cannot change and, therefore, we will only be defined by others. Then, we will be nouns in the eyes of others. But as long as we are alive we have the capacity to keep changing. That is an empowering and wonderful realization to hold onto as we proceed forward with our lives!

Because we live in a world that characterizes us as nouns and demands that we present ourselves as nouns, we are sorely tempted to defer to such categorization. When we believe that change is impossible, we do not have to face the struggle to overcome, to become better and to create a new and different life. It is scary and confusing to come to terms with the truth that 1) our past history describes us as nouns; 2) in the immediate moment we are verbs; and 3) at the termination of our lives we revert to being nouns. However, because we do live in the immediate moment we can only really be verbs, which means we fully know that we are capable of action or changing experience in the here and now. We essentially live in our own experiential reality even though others are most likely to see us only as existing in the world of objectively described reality. The individuals who recognize us as verbs will prove to be our most important friends and allies.

Lifting Anchor

We are certain of many things that we never question. For example, we know we exist. We also know when we have an itch, we know we have a hand to scratch that itch, and we know how to scratch. Such simple actions occur automatically without our needing to engage in any inner dialogue. In other words, we carry with us a basic sense of who we are and this implicit form of *knowing* is our inner compass. Immediate self-knowledge includes a recognition that we possess a bodily self, i.e., we have arms, legs, a mouth, etc. We also have a psychological self in that we see ourselves as shy or smart or clumsy or artistic or possessing any of a different number of qualities. It can be stated that we have a number of psychological selves insofar as the *me* who is a husband is in some ways different from the *me* who is a therapist.

Our bodily and psychological selves help us both to understand what is going on at any particular moment and to know how to behave in that situation. This fundamental sense of who we are orients us in basic ways to make sense of ourselves and our world. For example, individuals who define themselves as shy are not likely to approach a strange group of people standing ten feet away. Yet, other individuals who define themselves as socially popular are more likely to initiate social contact by walking over to these people. Certainly there will be times when the self-defined shy person will approach the group of strangers while the popular person will maintain personal distance. Nonetheless, the ways in which we see and define ourselves prompt us to engage in certain behavior patterns and avoid other actions. What we see and what we know dictates our understanding and our behavior.

Beyond the fact that we define ourselves in particular ways, we also carry with us certain mottos for living which we believe to be fundamentally true. Specifically, many of us consider the *Ten Commandments* to be universally valid principles for living. Virtually all of us also follow and endorse certain folk sayings such as *a stitch in time saves nine* or *haste makes waste* as desirable ways to behave. Basic beliefs or rules of living have become a routine part of our functioning without our having engaged in much, if any, rigorous self-questioning about the validity of these rules. Because we accept these principles as correct, we *know* how we are to behave. We assume that such *knowing* involves indisputable truths and our lives are much easier whenever we can find and endorse certain principles to guide our behavior.

We humans want and need to believe in permanent truths that we can use to define ourselves and which can also tell us what we should do. To *know* in such a basic and fundamental way is to experience a feeling of basic stability and safety. Such knowing gives us a feeling of solid footing for we will not be at a loss if we know who we are and what principles we need to use to guide our behavior. These supposed truths then become our personal anchors, for we all need something that can foster a greater sense of personal security.

However, whenever we let ourselves engage in serious self-questioning about what we believe, we ultimately come to the uncomfortable realization there are no such universally valid truths. As the old saying goes, "*the only thing you can be sure of is death and taxes.*" (We know some of us have even been able to avoid taxes.) As for death, while it is indisputably true we will all die, that piece of knowledge certainly does not provide us with any sense of security.

Consequently, the truths we create to make us feel better are, unfortunately, temporary and changeable conditions. Our rules must be subject to modification and, at times, suspension. *A stitch in time may save nine* but there are indeed times when one is better off waiting rather than taking any action. Maintaining a rigid belief in permanent truths without a willingness to modify one's position can prevent us from moving forward in our lives because it blocks us from making any significant personal changes. Although we all feel the need to know what is true and what is false, we can only know what is true for us at this particular moment in time. We must avoid treating certain personal beliefs as if they were indisputable truths. By adopting and maintaining certain truths, we create a helpful structure used to orient ourselves to the world. However, these personal truths constrict our experiences even though they simultaneously help us cope with the world.

For example, I have long maintained to everyone that I have no mechanical skills. I generally believe that I cannot fix things, and I typically avoid placing myself in positions where I attempt to do any repairs. I point out that when I took aptitude tests in elementary school, I scored in the lowest one percent in mechanical aptitude. Despite my belief that I am all thumbs, on occasion it actually has been necessary for me to fix certain things and I was amazed I had successfully repaired these objects. Obviously, my self-definition as a nonmechanical person has kept me from attempting certain activities. My belief in my lack of certain skills has made me avoid certain tasks because I was sure I would fail to complete them successfully. Even though this belief has kept me from attempting mechanical activities, by defining myself as all thumbs I have justifiably directed my energies to nonmechanical activities. I now recognize that I am not all thumbs, but I still do not wish to increase my involvement with mechanical projects. I maintain my public image as a man who is hopelessly inept with his hands. Furthermore, I have joked with friends that upon retiring from teaching I am considering becoming a handyman.

It has been necessary for me, just as it is for everyone else, to have a basic sense of my strengths and weaknesses. If I lacked such self-knowledge, I would be at a loss in deciding what to do and not to do. If in each situation, I still had to determine whether I was mechanical, artistic, intellectual, logical, empathic or equipped with any other well-defined talent, I could do no better than simply flip a coin to make my choice. We all need to have a sense of what our better skills and stronger interests are so we can make informed choices. Although this basic knowledge is very important, we also must recognize that skills, interests and talents can and do change. What is true for us today may not be true tomorrow. It is too constricting to expect that today's truth will be valid forever. If we remain open to change, we can learn skills we formerly thought were well beyond our capacities.

I recall counseling a 22-year-old man who was contemplating marriage. He said he would not marry anyone until he was sure he would still be happy with her after 25 years. Of course, no one can have such a guarantee. This particular man wanted certainties to make his life successful and consistently gratifying. We can all empathize with his wish because we all want to have meaningful, pleasurable and successful lives. Unfortunately, we can never ensure beforehand that we are making the right choices for a fulfilled life. If we demand a sense of certainty before taking action then we will basically remain immobile.

What we can instead hold onto are personal truths we believe are valid in the moment and will hopefully be true beyond that moment. The basic truths accepted by one person are likely to be very different from the basic truths endorsed by others. However, when you accept you are living your own truths at this particular moment, you are casting down your personal anchor in your own sea. I believe that seeing our lives as represented by a voyage over water is a useful analogy as water travel has important parallels to the course of life. When one sets sail in a pleasure boat, at times you simply continue to move ahead; at other times the sailor casts down the anchor and remains in the same place for a while. Similarly in our life voyage we need to be willing at times to lift anchor and chart a new course rather than attempt to stay fixed and unchanging. If one keeps the anchor in the water, the ship does not move forward. More importantly, if you are unwilling to challenge your truths of the moment and find new truths, you will not be able to move forward in life.

In our lifetimes we continually cast anchor, explore new territories and then lift anchor, move forward and explore the next territory. A ship's anchor needs to be lifted just as our truths need to be explored and sometimes altered. It may seem that our lives can proceed most simply if we maintain certain truths about oneself and do not change them over time. However, if the anchor always remains cast, the ship loses its purpose and identity as a ship. In a parallel fashion, to consistently avoid making changes in oneself is to avoid growth. The fact that we humans can and do change makes life very exciting and gratifying.

For myself in particular as I look back over time, I see that as a young man I rejected certain possibilities and concepts simply out of hand, just as I rejected the possibility I could effectively do anything mechanical. It would have been much more helpful to me if I could have seen that the truths I was endorsing then were subject to continued revision. When I found or created new anchors, I was readily convinced I then had hold of the real truth, instead of simply having created a new and still changeable set of beliefs. We all want and need to feel safe and secure. Anchors, or seeming indisputable truths, provide that illusion of security. However, we are safest when we are willing to raise the anchor and to dispute the validity of previously held truths.

I now realize that if, as a young man, I had viewed everything I believed in as being tentative, I might have been very frightened as I would not have been able to find something to provide stability. Then I did not realize I could gain some security by endorsing a belief in myself as a valid and changeable process. Such an idea would have been very foreign to me because it was extremely different from everything I had been taught. I very much wanted a sense of stability by holding onto the familiar because I knew I could function very well in dealing with the familiar. I did not trust that I could leap into new ventures and succeed. As a child and as a young man, I always entered the swimming pool by wading into the shallow end before swimming out to the deep end. I never liked simply to dive into the water.

During my lifetime I have become more comfortable in accepting and embracing change. I continue to like the familiar but I can also embrace the new. The analogy with the swimming pool still works well in describing my attitudes. I prefer wading to diving because I feel more vulnerable and at risk if I dive. Nonetheless, I choose to swim in deeper rather than shallower water.

Return to the analogy of life as a voyage on water. We are continually living in each moment and we must decide when to cast anchor and when to move forward. I often follow a momentary impulse in making such decisions. It would be comfortable to know when is the best time to change or the best time to remain stable and unyielding. Unfortunately, we cannot have such foresight and certitude, and often we can only trust in our impulse at the moment.

We can, however, maintain a willingness to embark on a journey of self-exploration and to actively raise the question of which truths to retain and which to discard. Young adults especially are at the perfect age to begin such a process of self-evaluation and discovery. As people move from late adolescence into adulthood, all the "truths" they were taught should be subjected to serious scrutiny. However, self-questioning and being open to change is a process that all of us need to continue as we progress through life. Particularly as many people enter the mid-life years, they realize the importance of reflecting backward on what has been accomplished in order to chart the course ahead. In our life voyage, we will have times of rough seas and will want to survive major storms. If we are open to seeing and exploring beautiful sights and do not get seriously "seasick," then we can feel very grateful for this voyage. We must, nonetheless, recognize that for all of us the life voyage will always pass through some unchartered waters. Such journeys can be perilous, adventuresome, awe inspiring, and very gratifying. Each of us must decide when to travel and when to hold on to the security of what is already known at that moment.

Objective and Subjective Realities

The first American psychologist, William James (1890), pointed out that the world is a buzzing, booming confusion to the infant. Such chaos is overwhelming, and the infant has to learn how to detect and decipher certain aspects of that massive stimulation in order to survive. She/he needs to know what a nipple is in order to be able to ingest food. He/she needs to be able to distinguish who is a mothering figure. Of course, the parents help the infant and the small child to make some sense out of all this confusion. They do so through direct and indirect teaching and by showing the infant what certain things are by name identification. This early form of learning focuses on teaching the children to know specific nouns. Young children are not taught the word *noun*, but they do learn the essence of what nouns are, i.e., stable and unchangeable phenomena. The child specifically learns who is mother and who is father. Mother must simply be *mother* for the small child; she cannot be a wife, a woman, a daughter or a big business executive. The idea of multiple identities is far too confusing as the infant needs simple anchors so that he/she can know that a person has only one identity. Therefore, *mother* is simply and universally mother. Only as the child matures can the child's mother assume different roles in the child's experiential world.

Small children need to acquire basic objective facts about their world. They need to know who they are, who their parents are, and what the world is like in order to orient themselves. Some label this knowledge as a cognitive structure; others call it a frame of reference. Both terms describe the basic ways in which one approaches the world. One of my professors, Milton Rokeach (1960), developed a theory of dogmatism which proposed the idea that all individuals had core beliefs. These beliefs included one's personal identity, i.e., one's name and one's ideas about the nature of the world, such as it is a friendly or unfriendly place. From these core beliefs we then all develop specific peripheral or consequent beliefs. For example, if we believe the world to basically be a friendly place, we would most likely develop the peripheral belief that it is better to reach out to neighbors than it is to keep to oneself. We approach, understand and interact with the world by drawing upon both our core and peripheral beliefs, which are our cognitive structure.

We acquire our core truths first through our dealings with our parents, and we then acquire a multitude of facts or other *truths* by spending time with other people and by attending school. The traditional primary task of education has been to make children knowledgeable and accomplished by instilling a multitude of facts. Presumably, the more schooling children receive, the more knowledge they will acquire. It is generally believed that increased knowledge makes us better educated people and more able to cope with life's demands.

Because such learning is both necessary and enormously helpful, it unfortunately can lead people to overvalue the importance of the ongoing acquisition of knowledge. Some people believe that the possession of sufficient facts is all that is necessary for effective and full survival in the world. As a child, I remember watching Dragnet, an early TV crime program which has recently been revived. The hero police investigator made a frequent comment when interrogating people by asking for *Just the facts ma'am.* What I am certain of is that *Just the facts* does not give us all the information we need. Eyewitnesses to the same event see it very differently. Consequently, the objective truth of what has happened is difficult if not impossible to discover. Nonetheless, many of us want to believe that *Just the facts* will answer all of life's questions and problems.

Another way of describing *Just the facts* is to speak of objective reality. The world of science focuses upon objective reality, and we need to understand and accept the validity of a consensual reality in order to survive. We need to know the rules of the road when we drive an automobile. Even more basically, we need to be able to identify what a vehicle is or else we may be killed. However, when we ask the question *Where shall I go in the car and how shall I get there*, we cannot find the answers through objective reality. A computer can provide a trip planner which specifies the quickest way to arrive at a particular destination, but it cannot choose the best destination. We can ask for suggestions from other people but the choice of what to do, how to do it and where to go ultimately remains our option and, hopefully, our joy. We also must recognize that we alone are responsible for our choices. Consequently, when it comes to making personal choices, the objective facts are insufficient as a guide.

Some people are deluded into believing that necessary objective facts are sufficient for decision making. Even though the trip planner specifies which interstate highway is the fastest route, one may still prefer to take back roads even though it means the trip will take a longer time. A choice to veer away from the time-saving route may still be a good choice. Those who like to *take time to smell the roses* need to be able to find a fragrant rose garden even if it is out of the way.

When we ascribe too much importance to objective truths, we may overlook the fact that we each have our own basic truths. Furthermore, these personal truths are different from the objective knowledge that we continue to acquire. We are all *knowers* insofar as we know ourselves and we *know* other people. Some of what we know is what we have accumulated from our prior learning. Other personal truths we are certain of are quite different from the objective facts that we were taught earlier. Furthermore, we can know things in a host of different ways. Sometimes we believe in unshakable truths which we consider to be of great importance. We may know other things only tentatively and consider these pieces of knowledge to be of little importance.

Our own personal reality consists of what we know and how we know it at each and every particular moment. Our personal reality can be, therefore, quite different from the objective truths that we were taught. How we react in each moment is then a consequence of this personal reality. Our personal reality is what we are experiencing and what we hold to be true. This form of knowing is more technically labeled as one's subjective reality.

To better understand the difference between objective and subjective reality, consider what happens when you read a newspaper. Most likely you read the paper selectively, beginning with the section you are most interested in, be it current events, business, sports, comics or entertainment. Some articles are read in depth, some skimmed over and still other parts of the newspaper are totally ignored. You do not simply process all the available information but instead you engage in a form of selective attention. Typically, after my wife and I have read the morning paper one of us will comment on an article and the other may very well ask *What are you talking about?* We both did not read the same articles. One of us ignored an article that the other found to be of interest. Thinking back to college, you may recall asking to borrow other students' class notes after you missed a particular class. When you read a few sets of notes, it appeared almost as if the students were not attending the same class because they each wrote down different parts of the lecture. These differences between what we see and read happen frequently enough to serve as a reminder that we are each very much engaged in our own personal realities.

Furthermore, when we take time to evaluate the information provided by our newspapers, we realize we are not simply reading objective facts. The editors of the paper decide which information is newsworthy, and the information deemed unnewsworthy is not included. The newspaper editors have selected the *important truths* which reflect their subjective decisions. The news we receive in American newspapers pays scant or no attention to much of what is happening in other countries. Only the most extraordinary foreign events are brought to our attention. In contrast with the newspaper readers in European countries, Americans appear to have a lessened sense of being part of an international community.

When we critically read newspaper articles, we realize the information is presented with a particular viewpoint. Editorializing is very much present in the news stories and is not confined just to the editorial and opinion pages. Our views of events are shaped by the supposedly objective reporters. It is important to acknowledge that we are influenced as well as informed each time we turn to the mass media for the news.

It would be preferable to be able to believe that the information we regularly acquire is *the truth.* Our lives would be much simpler if we did not have to continually evaluate each piece of information for validity. However, the real difficult truth is that whatever knowledge we acquire is incomplete; this knowledge has in part been acquired through dealings with other people who are invested in teaching us the "truth" as they themselves perceive it. Unfortunately, only a few people are committed to providing us with as unbiased a position as possible.

Even more problematic is that we all were taught in the earliest phases of our lives supposedly unquestionable truths as to what is *right* and what is *wrong*. We were given such information by parental figures as a necessary way of guiding our behavior. We needed to be given facts and rules as universal truths because as children we were not mature enough to consider information as being either partially true or partially false.

The most major truths, or rules for living, in the Judean-Christian tradition, are embodied in the Ten Commandments. While many adults do see these rules as good guideposts for living, they are not really inviolable, for it is considered ethically necessary to break these rules under certain circumstances. For example, *Thou shalt not kill* does not apply if your country is at war and you are a member of the armed services. The rule can be also broken if you kill in self-defense or in defense of your family, or if you are a member of the police, etc. As you see, these universal rules are not truly universal because they allow for exceptions. Societal standards do endorse the breaking of these commandments under specific conditions.

The existence of exceptions to rules makes it necessary for us to give greatest credence to our own way of seeing. We cannot simply and blindly apply these universal rules to all situations. When we give the greatest credence to our own decision-making processes, we affirm the importance of our own personal, subjective reality. The facts or data that we acquire in life are, of course, necessary for living; but we have to decide where and when they are to be used and where or when we should use our own subjective reality to guide us.

It is unfortunate that the formal education process typically places primary importance upon the acquisition of information and rarely advocates the importance of developing one's own values and one's own subjective reality. Our schooling too often teaches submission and conformity rather than encouraging individuality and the systematic questioning of the validity of all the information being taught.

Far too much of our educational processes treats the human being as an empty box to be stuffed full of information. This practice is essentially an endorsement of the 17th century philosophy of John Locke who believed that we are born with a blank mind that needs to be filled. It is, of course, vitally important to acquire certain information; but if the student is not encouraged to be a capable processor of information, the individual will be woefully inadequate as a decision-maker. I believe that too much classroom time is spent attempting to fill the student with important knowledge. As a result, with each year of ongoing education, the child can become overloaded with information. It is a fairly easy process to dispense information and to demand that the information be retained. To teach the integration, utilization and evaluation of additional knowledge would be a far more difficult task for educators to accomplish. However, the processing, utilizing and valuing of information determines which information becomes important and which is considered irrelevant and discarded.

What we experience and how we feel are the dimensions that give our lives personal value. Although we each process, evaluate or ignore information, the educative process rarely considers our own experiences to be central to our acquisition of knowledge. Without sufficient attention paid to the student as an information processor, learning is haphazard and problematic. I still remember the college welcoming speech given to my incoming class by one of the academic deans. He said that most of us had gone through high school learning to memorize that *ibble is bibble*. We were all very good at memorization, reflected in high grades which enabled us to be accepted by the University of Chicago. However, the dean told us that our college education was to be something quite different from rote memorization. We were to become fully engaged in evaluating and processing information rather than simple memorization. Classes would be discussion sections where we evaluated material rather than accept it on blind faith. Those first few college courses were a wonderful learning experience for me, and I regret that too few people are privileged to be taught in such a manner. I strongly believe that effective processing of information should be taught early in the educational process.

Especially important in the educational process is the degree to which we are able to use what we have learned. If, how, and when we use or discard information are the crucial processes that determine how we feel, behave and live. We are continually engaged in accepting, changing and discarding the information we have acquired. We are the judges and evaluators, and our evaluation process is what leads us to move our lives in particular directions. We need to pay special attention to how we actually make these decisions.

The formal learning process has been overvalued by many educators but without sufficient attention to the personal *knower* that we each are. Because our personal knowing has not been stressed by most authority figures, many of us essentially have learned to ignore ourselves as processes. It is very important, albeit difficult, to balance the value of objective facts with the necessity of engaging in subjective evaluations. We need to see ourselves as processors of information and to recognize that it is *what* we experience that must take precedence over the facts of objective reality. It is first, foremost and always our own personal reality that must be given the greatest importance. We all know far more than we give ourselves credit for knowing, and such "knowing" occurs in many other forms of life, much less complex than our own.

Knowing in Nature

Before I was a young adult I believed that reason and thinking were the most important tools we humans possessed. I did not reach this position independently for I, like most others, had been taught to regard humans as superior to all other forms of life. Human superiority was exemplified by our language and reason which set us apart from lower animals and made us the most special of species.

My graduate school training taught me a specialized professional language for understanding people and their problems. Because psychologists have become enamored of defining themselves as scientists, my training gave special attention to learning how to formulate rational hypotheses and how to design research studies to validate these formulations. We were taught that if one could not find or conduct research to establish the validity of any idea, then the idea should be considered too speculative to be of value. The primary focus of graduate school training in psychology, then and now, was to teach the student the *correct* ways of thinking and behaving. I had to learn various theories which all proposed the best ways to understand people. I also had to learn particular methods of speaking to patients, and too often the messages I received were about what *not* to say rather than what *to* say. In retrospect, I can see that the main training philosophy in my graduate school held too much in common with an assembly line where essentially naive students were shaped and transformed into thinking and behaving like "professionals." This basic philosophy of training was established long before behavior modification and cognitive behaviorism theories became the most popular methodologies for changing the thoughts and behaviors of human beings. To effectively navigate through graduate school, the student quickly had to become aware that professors each had their own ideas of what constituted the correct ways to think and behave. Students had to be able to alter their approaches and ideologies based upon which class they were enrolled in at that time.

Because I was invested in becoming a successful professional and had already been a very successful conformist (those good grades enabled me to enter a doctoral program), it was inconceivable for me to even contemplate that the most basic ideas of graduate training were in error. Doctoral programs are predicated on the assumption that reason and logical thinking are the key ingredients for mastering any discipline. I certainly do believe both reason and logic are very important ways of understanding. However, I now very much dispute that these rational approaches are indeed the primary tools we must draw upon to effectively understand and help other humans.

Earlier I explained that we can *know* and understand things as prereflective consciousness, which is a way of knowing before thinking. Specifically, when we *know* things as prereflective consciousness, we have an immediate understanding of what is most important in the particular moment. A similar kind of immediate knowing is present in other life forms. Both plants and animals *know* specific things that are vital for their survival. These forms of knowing cannot be labeled as thinking for we all acknowledge that plants do not possess a brain. While it is true that animals do have brains, they cannot match the human's capacity for thought as they do not have a highly developed cerebral cortex.

Nonetheless, what plants and animal do *know* is truly awesome. Any explanation which describes chemical receptors and genetic mutations as responsible for what and how animals and plants *know* does not provide me with an adequate explanation of their *knowing*. Take for example the recent devastating tsunami in southeast Asia that killed 200,000 people. Virtually all the animals in the region survived because they *knew* to move to higher ground before the tidal wave approached. I can further explain the nature of *knowing* by giving some examples of how my own pets have behaved.

I owned a dog and cat, Megan and Khafre, who grew up together as the best of friends and who both lived to be very old. After Khafre got run over by a car (and I believe he wanted that to happen as he had become very infirm), I proceeded to bury him in our back yard. Megan was kept in the house and could not see me carry the cat in a blanket and take his body to the rear of our property, nor could she see me digging the grave. Nonetheless, as soon as I began to dig, Megan started the most agonizing howling which she continued until the burial was completed. That was the only time in her life that Megan cried in such a manner. She would not venture to that spot in our yard for the rest of her life. The dog could not see what I was doing, and she did not possess thinking and logic as we know it, but she did have a very deep connection with Khafre.

A few years ago I read a book entitled *Dogs that know when their masters are coming home* (Sheldrake, 2000). This book details a number of experiments which demonstrated that particular dogs knew when their owners were first thinking about coming home even when they were thousands of miles away. Some dogs would also sense the moment of their master's death. In experiments cited by the author, some dogs were able to go home even if they were dropped off at an unfamiliar place. Other dogs knew when a human that they were closely connected to was about to have a heart attack. Because of this capacity for detecting beginning heart attacks, training programs have been developed for such dog companions. The main argument of this book was that dogs, and other species, can make a connection with another creature that enables them to transcend typical ways of knowing. The different experiments described in this book are all examples of knowing without thinking. It is quite astounding to learn what these animals have been able to know or apprehend.

Some humans also have powers of knowing that appear to go beyond the rational level of knowing. Some people know when the phone is about to ring and even who has dialed their number. These people do not experience this knowledge as a guess but are certain they know the caller even when the call is totally unexpected. We have all heard of people who know at the exact moment a close relative dies even when the relative is in another continent and the death is accidental. We currently have no way of understanding how this happens, but it certainly has happened too often to dismiss these anecdotes as chance occurrences. Many people would like to be able to find a scientific explanation for all these diverse phenomena rather than to admit there are forms of knowing we cannot explain. I personally am encouraged to hear that such unusual forms of knowing exist although I recognize there are charlatans who do make outlandish claims. Even some of these claims I believe are, indeed, valid.

Basic kinds of knowing are present in other life forms such as plants. When I study what is happening in my garden I recognize complex forms of knowing present in trees, flowers and plants. Consider what happens in the garden just before a storm arrives. Many trees and plants rotate their leaves so that it is the underside rather than the top side of the leaves which are pelted with water. Trees turn their leaves before the rain drops start to fall. Apparently they can detect rainstorms before they actually happen. Some flowers do exactly the same thing and close up so the rain does not destroy the blooms. These turnings and closings are acts of protection. The plants *know* when they have to protect themselves.

I am sure botanists can provide a biochemical explanation why these turnings and closings occur, but we are still left with the truth that the plant detects or knows the approach of danger. A similar predictive kind of knowing is present in many people who have arthritis or who had broken bones earlier in their lives. They, too, can tell you when a storm is about to happen. Is it, therefore, possible that these people developed a heightened form of awareness once they became injured? My own view is that they became able to know things in a more fundamental and primeval way because it became more imperative for them to become attuned to their bodies. After their injuries, they developed a way of knowing that most of us either once possessed and lost, or never acknowledged as a part of ourselves.

There are other forms of primitive knowing that one can detect in the garden whenever one engages in weeding. Some weeds seem to *know* the safest places to grow. Weeds with a particular kind of foliage will sprout up next to look-alike plants, i.e., plants that have a similar foliage. By finding safer places to grow, these weeds are more likely to escape detection and, therefore, survive. Of course not all weeds are that knowledgeable; yet it is amazing that a number of weeds seem to find the best ways to camouflage themselves. How can a seed have such knowledge? It seems beyond reason and yet it happens frequently. Is that not astounding? Consider too that one can fertilize and water one part of the garden and the plants do not thrive; yet, in another part of the garden where no fertilizer appears and no watering occurs, weeds grow unceasingly. Why? I also have read that some plants can send out messages, through the expelling of chemicals, to other plants when they are being attacked. These messages enable the other plants to utilize built in forms of self-protection. It seems to me that it is foolish to maintain the position that we humans are the only life forms that can know, anticipate and engage in self-protection, especially after we carefully study what happens with other forms of life.

I recently read *The botany of desire* (Pollan, 2001) which develops the idea that we humans are responding to what the plants want us to do, instead of vice versa. That is, the plants make themselves beautiful so that the bees will pollinate them and we humans will propagate these attractive plants. It is a very intriguing idea and somewhat humbling concept because it affirms the possibility that humans are not always the prime moving forces on earth. It is fascinating to consider the different kinds of knowing present in various life forms for it points to the possibility that we can expand our own understanding of the processes of knowing. Certainly there are instances of false knowledge, and no reliable method is currently available for tracking or systematically understanding how all forms of knowing exist. Nonetheless, it is apparent that forms of knowing exist in plants, animals and people quite different from the knowledge that is generated through rational thinking. I believe the reason these basic forms of knowing are present is in order to serve, protect and preserve the life of each organism.

Furthermore, I believe such forms of knowing are the manifestation of a fundamental life sustaining force present in all living things. This force is responsible for creating and furthering the existence of all life forms. I know this life force is incredibly powerful as it is quite obvious once you acknowledge the process of evolutionary growth on this planet. The recent advances in medical science have enabled us to significantly expand our life expectancy, but this science draws upon and strengthens our basic life force. It will indeed be wonderful when, if ever, we can better understand and connect with the basic life force that we all possess.

One very necessary manifestation of this life force is in the capacity to *know* and, correspondingly, to use this knowledge in order to sustain and protect the existence of the living organism. What is *known* or *knowable* by plants is much more limited than what is *known* or *knowable* by animals. The lower the animal is on the phylogenetic scale, the more limited is its capacity to *know*. It would, therefore, appear that humans would have the greatest capacity to *know*. Casual observation tells us that some people certainly *know* in full and deep ways, yet others seem to function quite poorly in their ability to *know*.

Most of us have been taught simply to develop our rational, thinking ways of knowing and not attend to or even seek out this more basic way of knowing. Those people who appear to *know* in the deeper ways utilize more than their capacity for reason in order to understand themselves and their world. We all possess the capacity to know in fuller ways by using both our prereflective consciousness as well as our reflective consciousness. One particular arena necessitates using both forms of consciousness in order to *know* and to be fulfilled. Most specifically we need to be able to *know* about other people. Actually, we all do *know* much more about others than we readily acknowledge. This form of *knowing* is typically labeled *knowing as the generalized other*. Because of its importance for our personal satisfaction and fulfillment, it warrants a separate discussion.

Knowing as the Generalized Other

The two basic ways of knowing are knowing through thinking (reflective consciousness) and immediate knowing without deliberate thinking (prereflective consciousness). Both ways of knowing draw upon the large fund of information or knowledge we have acquired over a lifetime, a fund of information you can liken to a database. Just as specific computer commands exist which provide immediate access to the database in the computer, our minds also appear to immediately retrieve information without following a consciously known system. We immediately know things at each moment, and we also assume that what we know is a consequence of having accessed the database of memory. Sometimes we use rational thinking as the way to connect to that database in order to know what is happening at a given moment. However, we are also able to connect with this database of knowledge through the process of feeling or what can be called *emotional knowing*. What we will ultimately know at any given moment is a consequence of using either thinking or feeling as our mechanism for accessing this data. More specifically, we will *know* different things based upon which method of access is used. A fuller description of the ways of knowing and the categories of knowledge that we have access to is described in *Inside clinical psychology; a handbook for graduate students and interns* (Potash, 1981).

The following example will better explain the distinction between rational and emotional knowing. Consider what happens when you are driving an automobile on the highway and another car darts in front of you. If you process what has happened, specifically by using rational thinking, you will immediately know this other person is a poor and reckless driver. That realization, in and of itself, is unlikely to lead you to take any particular action other than deciding to keep far away from that car. On the other hand, if you process what has just happened through the process of emotional knowing or feeling, you are likely to have a very different kind of experience. You might very well first feel afraid as you realize how close you came to having an accident. You might also feel very angry and start to curse the other driver. Hopefully, you will not decide to "teach that driver a lesson" and start a game of tag—a too common reaction among drivers who suffer from road rage.

People vary in the frequency with which they use thinking or feeling to understand their world. Not only do these methods lead to profoundly different kinds of knowledge, but also the very experience of what you know becomes diversified as well. Neither thinking nor feeling can be categorized as the best way of processing information, for at times each method is better and more helpful and sometimes we may know by using both thinking and feeling simultaneously. However, in all cases we simply and immediately have the experience of *knowing what we know* without deliberately choosing one method of knowing over another. What we are able to do, after the fact, is to review what has occurred and to determine which particular method of knowing we have utilized. Engaging in such a process of evaluation allows the individual to decide, through rational thinking, whether the used method, i.e., the process of thinking or feeling, was indeed the better way for accessing one's database of knowledge.

The core of our database of knowledge was acquired through dealings with parents, teachers or other authority figures. When individuals assume the role of authority, it is quite common for them to demand that their audience attend to and accept their information as valid. Consequently, this form of authoritative influence has led many individuals to believe what they have learned through the voice of others is more important than what they may be able to learn through trial, error and personal experience.

However, the practical knowledge we acquire as we navigate through the world has taught us how to survive and sometimes even thrive in a difficult and complex environment. This kind of practical knowing is of crucial importance although many do not give it sufficient credit. We often de-emphasized its value because we were taught that personal experience is not as helpful or useful as the knowledge gained through formal training. As stated earlier, many authorities themselves give little credence to personal experience, so it is quite difficult for others to believe that their own personal experience offers their most important compass. I believe that the personal experiences we gain through daily living provides us with the most valuable knowledge. When we can trust in this form of knowing, we will be most successful and most fulfilled.

The practical knowledge we have acquired through living in a social world and dealing with other people on a daily basis has made most of us adept at reading and understanding others. Sullivan (1950) specified that people can and do use words both to communicate and to deceive others. When we listen, we not only attend to what is said, but often we also listen for what is not said. Furthermore, we pay careful attention to the tone, style and inflection of the other's speech. We implicitly know we have to recognize and look for nonverbal cues such as how others dress, how they position and present themselves, as well as their facial expressions. We understand others at a much fuller level by reading their verbal and nonverbal cues. It is interesting, however, that even though most of these strategies for knowing and understanding other people are part of our personal data bank, few of us spontaneously acknowledge that we regularly process and use this information in our interpersonal transactions.

These strategies and principles for understanding others enable us immediately to know their emotional states. We quickly recognize different signs which inform us of anger, anxiety, happiness or disinterest. Many of us are so proficient at reading the emotional state of others that we are able to fully trust in this form of *knowing*. Our ability to read other people is a product of our formal and informal learning and is also a consequence of our past experiences in dealing with others.

This ability to know or to *read* other people is acquired because in our culture, just as in all other cultures, specific behaviors are given particular meaning. We have been taught that when we want to make a positive impression, we should attend to our clothes, voice tone and certain nonverbal gestures. In other words, we have learned the importance of impression management. We immediately know others are not interested in creating a positive impression when they do not try to present themselves in a favorable light. Such behavior can be caused by a wide variety of reasons, e.g., depression or anger, low self-esteem or ignorance. Despite the hypothesized causes, we cannot ignore that the person is not interested in making a positive impression.

We also detect when others are anxious, depressed or angry by the specific manners in which they carry themselves. Posture and voice tone are often better indicators of emotional states than are actual words. The ability to detect others' intentions is a very important survival mechanism, and most of us are quite adept at it. Some people skilled at reading other people's body language can use the information for destructive purposes. Specifically, it has been documented that many rapists study the ways in which women walk in order to detect who is passive and unlikely to fight back.

When I taught courses in personality assessment, I explained how verbal and nonverbal cues provide important information. The ways people shake hands, the types of eye contact, their ability to smile, their voice tone and general demeanor all provide significant information. We use that data to decide who is self-confident or assertive or timid. However, in our daily living we rarely if ever have occasion to specify the techniques and data we use to understand other people, even though it is very important and reassuring to recognize that we know far more about others than we care to admit.

The ability to deeply *know* what the other person's feelings and intentions are can be our most trustworthy barometer, as it informs us whom to approach and whom to avoid. For example, I believe that most people would readily agree as to who is acting silly or who is generally undesirable or offensive. We can also easily detect who is emotionally warm and who is emotionally cold as we all emit many cues without always being aware of the transmitted information.

In my personality assessment classes I asked students to create a complete personality profile based upon knowledge of a specific behavior. For example, students were asked to speculate what other behaviors they would expect from someone who tried to avoid making eye contact. They were asked to imagine how such a person would behave if on a date or attending a party or working as an employee or functioning as a parent. When class members voiced their ideas, they soon recognized they had quickly reached a consensus of opinion about the hypothetical person. They agreed that lack of sustained eye contact reflected a timidity or lack of assertiveness which would be expected to extend to a whole host of behavior patterns. In other words, they realized that one small piece of behavior was very likely connected with a whole range of behaviors and personality styles. Most human beings know this to be implicitly true, but few people have been asked to verbalize these conclusions and consequently are usually unwilling to trust this form of knowing.

Our feelings toward other people are rarely unique, for the people that we like will most typically be liked by most others. In parallel fashion, the people we dislike will, no doubt, be disliked by most others. Because of our common culture, we respond positively to culturally desirable behaviors and negatively to culturally undesirable behaviors. Psychologists describe common reactions to other people's specific behaviors as a result of the truth that we all function as the *generalized other*. Because we are members of a society or a subgroup sharing certain values and standards, we have common reactions to specific actions. When I personally recognize that another person is menacing, I can trust that *most* people will have the same reaction when facing such behavior. When I see another person's demeanor as depressed, I am sure that others will see this depression as well. My personal reactions are usually the same as other people's reactions and in that sense, I can and need to trust my personal reactions. We *know* other people because of the common ways in which we communicate; the behaviors that we are reading have particular meanings.

Because we each will usually have the same reactions to certain behaviors, this knowledge can help us to trust that our own feelings and reactions are usually quite valid. If an individual makes you uncomfortable or angry, it is likely that most other people would have the same reaction to such a person. In a similar way, when you find another person to be interesting and appealing, chances are this individual is seen in a positive light by most others as well. Our reactions to other people reflect our immediate and intuitive *knowing*. As such, they provide us with vital information which can be used both for self-protection and for self-enhancement. Again, this immediate knowing, the knowing as the generalized other, is a vital and important method for effective relationships with others.

Sometimes we are very uncomfortable and uneasy in the presence of a particular person. We all especially need to be able to trust that our discomfort exists for a very good reason. There have been two specific occasions in my life when I was in the company of a person whose voice tone and demeanor scared me. Both were patients hospitalized on a psychiatric unit, and my emotional reaction was not connected to any particular words that the patient was saying. However, I knew I wanted to be out of that person's presence very quickly, and it would have been very foolish for me to mistrust that feeling. Subsequently, I discovered that one of those patients had intended to commit random murder.

I believe our capacity to immediately know that another person is dangerous to us parallels the self-protective instincts of other animals who are able to smell or sense that danger is coming. If those animals had to check out the validity of their reactions by engaging in rational thinking, they would probably be killed. They do not have the luxury of extra time for self-preservation. Unfortunately, too many humans do not trust their own immediate form of knowing and as a result often are mistreated or victimized.

Many people first learned to mistrust their immediate way of knowing when they were young children. Often, in their family of origin, a powerful parental figure did not want the child to see or know the truth of what was happening in the household. This denial is all too common in families where one parent is an alcoholic. In such families the other parent often refuses to acknowledge that the spouse is drunk and out of control. The child, on the one hand, knows the parent is irrational and drunk but simultaneously is not allowed to believe, or at least is not allowed to say, that the parent is drunk. Consequently, when children in these families must deny the truth of their perceptions, a pattern is established which will persist through much of their lives. They will continue to mistrust what they implicitly know. Unfortunately, the problem of not trusting what one knows is not confined to the families of alcoholics but happens in too many other families as well.

The central destructive phenomenon is that parents in such unhealthy families do not validate the perceptions of the child. Accordingly, even though the child is basically equipped to be able to *know* in a basic and full way, the parents block the child from trusting this way of knowing.

The child is forced to defer and, consequently, is deprived of a basic survival skill.

A large number of my therapy patients have suffered from an inability to trust what they know, and this personal mistrust caused many problems for them in daily living. Most people will experience some difficulty in fully trusting what they know, especially if it does not come from reflective consciousness. However, the degree of self-mistrust varies enormously among people and is a consequence of one's early upbringing. I strongly believe that being able to trust in our immediate knowing is the best guide to living. I do not dispute the importance of the knowing that comes through thinking, but rationally based knowledge does not enable us to make important personal choices about relationships.

Because at times we mistrust our immediate form of knowing, many of us turn to others for suggestions and guidance. However, this is usually a form of self-deception. When we turn to others for advice, we usually ask several people for suggestions until someone provides the advice we originally wanted to hear. That particular suggestion seems correct because it fits with what we want to hear. By attributing the source of the correct idea to another person, we can falsely believe the choice was made for us instead of recognizing that we ourselves are the essential choosers. In such a way we disown the responsibility for the choices.

Yet in such instances, we all remain responsible for having asked and for having believed in what the other person said. Obviously, it simply would be better to trust in our own immediate form of knowing. No one else can know what is better for each of us than we know ourselves. Nonetheless, our schools do not teach us to trust in our knowing as prereflective consciousness. For many, the early upbringing and education has invalidated our personal *knowing*.

We possess many different ways of immediately *knowing*, and we vary considerably in the degree to which we can trust in what we know. At specific times we may fully trust what we know and at other times we may fully lose sight of what we basically know. Our immediate ways of knowing include knowing about others, as the generalized other, but it also involves our capacity to know what to do in order to be effective with other people. Such forms of knowing are an outgrowth of being centered in ourselves in a positive way. Certainly we are not omniscient; and we are far from being all-knowing for there will be times when we are at a loss as to what to do and where to go.

We all can be victimized by a destructive internal force that, at times, prevents us from being able to *know* and to trust in this knowledge. This basic and powerful fundamental force can block our immediate knowing and create enormous misery and trouble. I label this force as the unhealthy side of our personality. In order to be able to counteract this unhealthy side of the personality, it is necessary to understand both how it functions and how it develops— the topics of the next two sections.

The Healthy and Unhealthy Sides of our Personality

Everyone who wants to become healthier has to be able to understand the forces that block them from forward movement. In order to develop greater self-control, people need to have a fuller understanding of how their minds work. We need to recognize the presence of positive and negative forces within us. Most of us have come to trust that what we think and what we feel are accurate and valid ways of knowing. It is understandable that we trust whatever is going on in our heads because otherwise we would feel immobilized. Yet we all do know there have been times that our thoughts and feelings were very inaccurate. No intruder was actually in our house, even though we heard a sound. Or later we discover that we misheard or misunderstood another person. We thought one thing was being said but a totally different message was being communicated. In other words, we know that sometimes our thoughts, senses and feelings are wrong. Much of what we experience, however, must be trusted because we cannot function if we mistrust all of our perceptions. On the other hand, we also have a certain cluster of thoughts and feelings which we need to be able to question and to overcome. Occasionally you have experienced strange thoughts and fantasies which you wish would never have happened. This kind of experience is common to us all. But sometimes these uncomfortable experiences are part of a larger pattern, and it is that pattern which warrants further explanation.

As you well know, we all acquire various skills as we progress through the phases from infancy into adulthood. Unfortunately, the capacity to be able to step outside one's own experiences and effectively evaluate oneself and gain personal insight does not develop until late adolescence. Children at earlier ages are certainly very much aware of themselves, and in the early years of adolescence they are often very preoccupied with what and how they are feeling. However, it is only in late teens that they can make more objective evaluations and begin to understand the complexity of their mental processes. Elementary school children certainly can have a very good idea of their preferences as well as their strengths and weaknesses; but it would be extremely unlikely for them to be able to understand why they have these particular tendencies. Children, just like adults, have many different thoughts and feelings which seemingly appear at random. A number of these thoughts can be negative and cause great discomfort. It then becomes important to account for these uncomfortable feelings in order to gain mastery over potentially destructive mental processes.

During late adolescence many people first begin some form of self-analysis whereby they try to figure out how and why they have developed in particular ways. Such self-questioning is an intriguing, sometimes awful and oftentimes wonderful process. This process of self-evaluation is conducted by a part of the personality that is commonly called the observing ego. The purpose of the observing ego is to look at ourselves rationally—to see what we are doing and decide whether it makes good sense. The observing ego can evaluate in the immediate moment as well as look back in time and evaluate past behaviors. The observing ego functions similarly to the actions of the judge in a courtroom; judges listen, evaluate and make final decisions.

Although many of us are primarily concerned with evaluating our outward behaviors, we also can profit from trying to understand and evaluate internal feelings and experiences. How we think, feel and make judgments is, in large part, a consequence of our past associations with other people. Parents, siblings and other relatives become heavily engaged in showing us how to be and how not to be, starting very early in our lives. We all have been directed to think and to feel in particular ways. We have been taught what is good and what is bad. These early teachings are an important part of our own thoughts and feelings as we proceed through life. We all would like to believe these thoughts and feelings are simply all our own, but that cannot be true. Many of our ways of experiencing were guided and directly learned. Each of us also experiences some specific ways of viewing the world in direct reaction against what we were taught. For example, if we were raised by a stingy parent, some of us vow to become generous. In similar fashion, some children of prejudiced parents often assume quite liberal and nonjudgmental positions regarding others. We have all been heavily influenced by other people as part of the socialization process. However, the task we must face is being able to decide which influences we wish to keep and which ones we wish to discard.

As a first step toward acquiring personal independence, many adolescents routinely reject all parental standards. Yet, at the same time, they experience many contradictory thoughts and feelings. Trying to decide which impulses, thoughts and values are personally correct and which are to be discarded is a task that only begins in adolescence. It necessarily continues as we grow and mature in life.

We all are familiar with the presence of conflicting wishes or thoughts. It has been elegantly described in different comic strips. We see a figure who is trying to decide on a course of action with a picture of both a devil and an angel, each trying to convince the person to follow a particular action. In most comic strips the issue is whether the devil or the angel wins out and, thereby, leads the figure to engage in either bad or good behavior. We are all personally familiar with having ambivalent feelings like wanting to go out to have fun and at the same time wanting to accomplish important, pressing chores.

Involved or caring parents repeatedly tell their children what is acceptable and unacceptable behavior. Children quickly learn so they become aware that some things they might want to do are *bad* and will get them into trouble. Of course, they also could quickly learn which things they might want to do that are *good*, which will bring them praise and reward.

Children raised by basically emotionally healthy parents will be taught to behave in ways leading them to become emotionally healthy adults. In such families, children are indeed taught positive skills that will lead them to success. In the course of effective socialization, the child will desire to do the good things that will spell interpersonal success. But certainly by the time children reach adulthood, they will quite likely disagree with some of these parental standards and rules. If children remain in total agreement with everything their parents endorsed, then as adults they will fail to develop their own separate, independent points of view.

Beginning in early childhood we learned of the impulses or urges that are good for us and that lead to praise and reward. We have also learned that certain impulses or urges are bad for us to follow for they lead to trouble. All of us have both kinds of urges. I refer to these two kinds of urges as expressing the healthy and unhealthy sides of our personality.

We all know, for example, that exercise is good. When we do not want to exercise, it is the unhealthy side of our personality that is doing the "talking." Every time we relinquish self-control and act in ways that are opposed to our best interest, it is the unhealthy side of our personality dominating our behavior. When, as a student, you give yourself enough time to study for an exam, the healthy side of your personality is in control. At work, when you take the time to address your tasks thoroughly and completely, it is, again, the healthy side of your personality guiding your actions. When you fail to go to the library before closing time or forget to pay your bills, then the unhealthy part of your personality is in control over your behavior.

When I describe the actions of the unhealthy side of our personality to my clients, I prefer to label the unhealthy side as *it*. I choose that term deliberately because the unhealthy side generates awful, uncomfortable and sometimes disgusting thoughts. Although these mental images are totally opposite to the ways the healthy side of our personality works, we can, nonetheless, be plagued by such negative thoughts. We all need to be able to understand why we have impulses we find abhorrent. The simplest, and I believe most correct, explanation for such terrible thoughts is that a part in each of us works against our best interest. Because at heart we are most fundamentally represented by the healthy side, we have to renounce the unhealthy side by calling it alien to whom we really are. One way to do so is by labeling the unhealthy side as *it*.

Often it is very difficult to decide if the healthy or unhealthy part of your personality is dictating behavior. The unhealthy side can be brilliant or devious because it is a part of a very smart brain. It can argue that you were really too tired to prepare properly and that "preparation" will not really matter. Unhealthy sides are capable of rationalizing or excusing behavior that is not in our best self-interest. Both the healthy and unhealthy parts of your personality will use reason to advocate their points of view, which means very clever arguments can be created both for your best interests and against them.

One's unhealthy side may argue that you have been "too good," that you need to unwind and relax and not take life so seriously. This wise-sounding argument can, indeed, be valid unless one chooses to relax at a time that will cause serious trouble. Most of us have at one time or another attempted to diet. When we see a piece of our favorite dessert, we *hear* the thought of how delicious the dessert would be. However, the healthy side can and will tell us to wait for some weeks before our weight will allow us to have that dessert. It is a very familiar struggle. We are regularly pulled in opposite directions by the healthy and unhealthy sides of our personality, and each of us differs in the relative strength of these two sides of our personalities.

The power of the unhealthy side of the personality is quite evident when we attend to the range of different behaviors people exhibit. Forgetting to do a small chore represents a minor triumph of our unhealthy side. Practicing unprotected sex is a wholly different and much more serious matter, demonstrating a powerful urge to be in very serious jeopardy. When one behaves in such a self-destructive manner, you can detect strong evidence that the unhealthy side of the personality is, indeed, very powerful and vicious. It is obviously imperative that the unhealthy side of the personality be curtailed. However, the first step is to acknowledge that the unhealthy side of the personality has been in control.

These few examples are designed to demonstrate that simple rebellion against parental rules can be quite mild when compared to possible tactics directed by the unhealthy side of the personality. Self-destructive behaviors, such as illegal drug use or alcohol abuse, are always a manifestation of the unhealthy side of our personality. Behavior in our own best interest represents the actions of the healthy side of the personality.

When people have major psychological problems it is usually because the unhealthy side of their personality has become too powerful. They behave in response to their unhealthy instead of their healthy side. In fact, the loud and seemingly automatic desires these people experience can and will emanate from their unhealthy side. Most importantly, and unfortunately, these individuals are unaware of the source of these ideas. When I work with psychotherapy patients, my aim is to strengthen their healthy sides and to help them to recognize and diminish the power of their unhealthy sides.

Obviously it is vitally important for the healthy side of the personality to be in control of one's actions. When the unhealthy side assumes dominance, the individual needs to gain healthy control either through ongoing self-reflection or by seeking professional help to strengthen the healthy side. I strongly believe increased self-awareness provides the best route to mental health, enabling us to live rewarding and successful lives. Everyone, psychotherapy patient or not, needs to be aware of the presence of both the healthy and unhealthy side of the personality. Not only must we all be aware that we have an unhealthy side, but we also must learn exactly how that unhealthy side operates.

Individuals who effectively direct their lives are able to trust they will routinely act out of their healthy side. Therefore they can be guided by their immediate form of knowing. When the unhealthy side is quite powerful, then one is unable to routinely trust that this knowing represents basic self-interest. In such instances it is vitally important to begin questioning and monitoring one's thoughts and emotions.

In order to detect the operation of the different sides of our personality, we need to frequently ask ourselves, *Is what I want to do now coming out of my healthy or my unhealthy side?* Being able to ask that question becomes an action taken by your observing ego, and through the question you are invoking and strengthening that observing ego. Not only have you engaged in self-monitoring but also you can evaluate and ultimately choose the best and healthiest course of action. The simple act of stopping and asking which part of your personality is speaking is a very empowering experience. By determining which part is in control at a particular moment, you ultimately become able to shift the balance of power from the unhealthy to the healthy side of the personality.

We all wish that no part of us will operate against our basic self-interest. However, such is not the case; and we are best served by recognizing we must be alert to our own negative tendencies. We can easily look at others and see how frequently they act in self-defeating ways. These self-destructive behaviors are a consequence of the power of their unhealthy sides. Because so many people act in ways that hurt themselves, we have to acknowledge that all of us have the capacity to be controlled by our unhealthy sides. The best protection against self-deception is the recognition that we can be easily tricked by our unhealthy sides. We must consider whether we have engaged in any negative behavior in order to prevent a repetition of self-destructive behavior. Such self-questioning is an excellent way to re-establish the power of the healthy side of the personality.

The healthy side provides the immediate, intuitive knowing that promotes growth and leads toward meaningful, productive and satisfying choices. The unhealthy side of the personality acts as an enemy. It often ridicules and attacks a positive self-image. It argues against healthy choices and promotes self-doubt. It leads people into a full range of self-abusive behaviors such as addictions, co-dependency and self-mutilations. It propels us into relationships that can undermine self-confidence and cause harm in countless physical and psychological ways.

Unless people actually acknowledge both healthy and unhealthy forces in their personalities, they can easily be misguided by their unhealthy sides. If you do not realize that some of your thoughts come from your unhealthy side, you will fail to recognize the necessity of monitoring and challenging these ideas and impulses. Remember, the unhealthy side of your personality can use your basic intelligence to advocate against you. Therefore, one part of you is as capable of arguing against yourself as you are capable of following your own best interests.

When the healthy side of your personality is very strong, the act of questioning is sufficient for you to recognize which thoughts are self-affirming and healthy. Correspondingly, it will be possible for you to recognize which thoughts are self-negating and self-attacking. Once you have such awareness, you are able to choose to follow the healthy side of your personality. However, for people whose unhealthy side is very powerful, it is difficult to recognize, monitor and conquer the unhealthy side. These individuals can profit by entering into psychotherapy as the struggle between the healthy and unhealthy sides of the personality is often too difficult to win without outside assistance.

When we recognize the presence of unhealthy messages and thoughts and are then able to counteract them, we are doing something very important for ourselves. Specifically, we have used our *will* to move our lives in a positive direction. We need to exercise our *will* when we become aware of the unhealthy components to our personality pulling us in hurtful ways. Without clear recognition of the unhealthy side of one's personality, there is no perceived need to use one's *will*. As long as one remains unaware of this internal destructive force, we can be deceived which, in turn, leaves the unhealthy side in control. Monitoring and evaluating one's thoughts and experiences is an important way to expand one's self-awareness, thereby enabling one's *will* to exercise its best judgment. By strengthening your *will* through increased self-knowledge, it becomes much more possible for the healthy side of your personality to take fuller control of your behavior.

Creating and strengthening the alliance between the *will* and the healthy side of the personality has been the central focus of my professional work as a psychotherapist. This alliance, while being the central key to effective psychotherapy, is also vitally important for all humans, whether or not they ever enter a psychotherapist's office. Using our *will* to follow the healthy side of our personality is the key to effective and meaningful living. All individuals can strengthen this alliance to some degree even without a therapist's help. Keep asking yourself which "side" of you is talking, and you will find yourself increasingly empowered.

The Development of the Unhealthy Side of our Personality

My years as a psychologist have affirmed for me the crucial importance of understanding our own personal developmental history. We need to recognize the important milestones in our early lives which have made us move in particular directions as well as the particular events which have helped shape our personality. This kind of understanding is labeled insight. When we gain such insights, we increase our power to be able to recognize and eliminate our unhealthy behavior patterns. Insight is particularly important whenever we have adjustment problems as it helps us discover the root causes of these problematic behaviors. When you want to understand your strengths and weaknesses or how you came to be who you are now, it is helpful to review personal history, seeking to understand the positive and negative influences of major life events. That kind of exploration is usually conducted with a psychotherapist, although a person can gain many of these insights independently. I hope to be of assistance here by providing a model of how both the healthy and unhealthy sides of the personality develop. In turn, this information may better point the way for you to identify whatever unhealthy tendencies are present.

Each of us has an unhealthy side in our personality, and it arises in the natural course of human development. All infants function as a mass of diffuse urges as babies are unable to identify their specific needs at any particular time. Nonetheless, infants do have a well known method of communicating their neediness or discomfort which is, of course, by crying. The infant's cries usually catch the attention of parental figures who then attempt to decipher and satisfy the baby's needs—for example, discover if the baby is hungry, wet, overstimulated, tired, sick, etc. Parental figures cannot immediately detect the specific needs, but the healthy and loving parent will ultimately discover what the child needs and then provide it.

Parents are inescapably human. They cannot always be other-centered and at times may wish to satisfy their own personal needs instead of continually attending to the needs of a baby. Even though healthy parents recognize these longings, they are usually able to suspend personal needs because they recognize the needs of the dependent baby are far more pressing. When a parent possesses a very powerful unhealthy side in his/her personality, it becomes much more difficult to place the needs of the child before personal needs. Even when such parents are able to outwardly satisfy the baby's needs, their personal resentment is quite likely expressed through bodily tension. At other times their resentment may be shown by providing only a minimal level of necessary care.

Even the healthiest and most loving parent is at times very frustrated with a crying, needy baby. In particular, colicky infants will continue to cry despite any or all of the parent's interventions, thereby raising the parent's stress level. Whenever parents become sleep deprived, their frustration tolerance is lowered. In addition, the parents may also be dealing with other personal frustrations which will make it more difficult to effectively focus upon satisfying the needs of the baby.

As babies mature, some of their behaviors will generate stress and frustration in the parents. For example, the baby begins to explore the world by putting any and all objects into her/his mouth. Everything may be put in the mouth whenever the small child remains unsupervised. The attentive parent safeguards the child by insuring that dangerous objects are kept out of reach so they cannot be swallowed. The child's exploration of the world through the mouth is necessary and healthy, but careful parental intervention is even more necessary as the baby must be protected. In these early transactions the parents first give the message that some things are good for the baby and other things are bad.

We can easily recognize when the baby wants to do something that may be harmful. Accordingly, the parent begins to teach the child that some wishes are not good, i.e., these actions undermine the child's best interests, while other wishes are very much in the child's best interest. You can see that the seeds of the healthy and unhealthy personality are first sown in this initial conflict between parent and baby.

However, most of what the baby or young child wants to do is in the child's best interest. The child needs to walk and to talk and to see and understand the world. These actions must be taken as the child moves toward becoming a capable person. When the healthy sides of the parents are strong, then it is quite natural for the parental figures to be positively invested in helping the child systematically reach for greater independence and understanding.

However, far too many parents cannot accept the child's burgeoning independence and they may block and interfere with this process. Some parents are fearful and keep the child too close to them out of misguided love. They may withdraw their attention and affection whenever the child makes independent moves. In such encounters the child is being taught not to move in healthy directions. Accordingly, these children will eventually abandon or compromise their healthy tendencies and instead follow the parental dictate which requires pleasing the parent rather than oneself. This negative message becomes the core of the unhealthy side of the personality.

Quite early in life children will begin learning not to follow their healthy or life-affirming tendencies. In so doing the unhealthy side of their personality becomes strengthened. Certainly the healthy parent needs to intervene and stop the child from engaging in destructive behavior. However, the caring parent hopefully will not block the child's healthy tendencies. When the parent interferes with the normal life-affirming tendencies in the child by keeping the child too sheltered, then the unhealthy side of the child becomes stronger.

When parents have major emotional problems, the unhealthy side dominates their own personality. As a result, they often deal with their children from their unhealthy rather than their healthy side. For example, they may not want their child to recognize some basic facts about what is happening in the family, such as a parent is drunk or abusive or irrational. When they do not allow the child to recognize these ugly truths, they also are able to keep blocking themselves from accepting these truths as well. As another example, if parents have major difficulty in tolerating anger, they can teach the child to suppress angry feelings. In so doing they are advocating that their children function out of their unhealthy sides.

The more the parent cannot allow the child to become a successful and independent person, the more the parent is encouraging and strengthening the unhealthy side of the child's personality. In some instances the destructive parental pressure can become so great that the children have great difficulty in even knowing what their healthy tendencies are. It is certainly quite understandable why such people would have major problems in being able to succeed in the world.

In my early training as a psychotherapist, most of the professional writings de-emphasized the frequency and depth to which parents can interfere with healthy development of their children. Most mental health professionals recognized that a very small percentage of parents had caused their children's emotional problems, but the depth of the destructiveness was minimized in too many other instances. For example, I was told to anticipate that therapy patients would pass through a stage of rebellion against their parents. This rebellion was to be expected and normal because, it was assumed, that the parents had specific goals for the child (and now the adult) that were at variance with what the child (now adult) wanted. After the rebellion stage in therapy, a reconciliation with parents was expected and was to be encouraged. Use of this strategy assumed that parents always had the child's best interests at heart. It was expected that over time the parents would see the wisdom of the child's (now adult's) new direction. Because basic and healthy love was assumed to be present, that love was expected to win over both parents and children.

In my psychotherapeutic practice many patients described so much destructive and hateful parental behavior that often a positive reconciliation was not deemed possible. Most specifically, it violates basic human nature for children or adults to forgive the parent who sexually molested them. They cannot forgive the parent who administered daily or weekly beatings because the parent needed to find an outlet for out-of-control rage. The damage these parents did to their children was so deep and far reaching that it had created powerful and unhealthy sides within the children's personalities. Once these unhealthy tendencies were established, the acquired unhealthy side of the child's personality functioned as viciously to the child/adult as the parent had once treated that child. The internalization of the destructive parent and the destructive messages of that parent then became the unhealthy side of the child/adult personality.

Certainly, all children will at times be in conflict with their parents. The conflict can be as simple as the child wanting to spend more time with friends and the parent wanting the child to come home and eat dinner. In this kind of minor conflict the child usually has to conform to the parental demand. Such a demand for compliance in and of itself is not a problem. However, this example serves to remind us that parents and children often do have healthy but conflicting needs, and positive resolutions are not always easy or possible.

In those families where neither parent is willing or able to assist primarily in the child's growth and development, the child is forced continually to submit to parental dictates. If the parent is threatened by the child's growth or requires the child to forever remain dependent or subservient, then the child will develop difficulties likely to persist throughout life. Children will learn it is dangerous to develop their healthy side, and therefore the self-punitive or unhealthy side of their personality will become dominant. As a basic survival mechanism, such children learn to block their own healthy development and impede their personal growth.

Through childhood and into adulthood the attacking voice of the parent becomes very familiar to the individual; these internalized messages sound *right* and quite likely remain unchallenged. As a result, the victims of such verbal abuse treat themselves in the same way that they had been treated by the parent. Unless they become aware of how *wrong* these messages are, they are likely to respond to their own children in the very same manner. In such fashion the cycle of abuse becomes perpetuated.

This pattern will ultimately persist throughout a lifetime unless or until he/she becomes fully aware of this unhealthy side. He/she needs to become aware of when and how that unhealthy side operates. People also need to recognize their own immediate tendencies to block personal development as arbitrarily malicious re-enactments of the parent's behavior. When the unhealthy side of the person is very strong, it will be extraordinarily difficult for that person to be able to counteract and overcome these destructive tendencies.

Because perfect parents and a perfect world do not exist, we all have an unhealthy side to our personalities. The size and power of this unhealthy side is primarily a consequence of the kind of treatment received from one's parents. Even so, we all experience some thoughts or urges that are not in our own best interests. We all have thoughts, temptations or impulses which, if followed, would create significant personal problems. By finding the roots of these urges, one becomes better able to counteract them.

Self-questioning produces insight, and insight leads to heightened personal power. We each are fully capable of knowing what is best for us and what is not. With this knowledge we can exercise our *will* to act in ways that further develop our healthy sides. Self-questioning is very hard and demanding work, but it helps us take fullest control of our lives. Believe in the old adage *knowledge is power.* If I did not have such a belief, I would have no reason for writing this book.

Being Plumb

For the major part of every day, we individuals *know* in the most basic ways who we are, what is going on, and what we must do about what is happening around us. This kind of *knowing* is so immediate and so trustworthy that we do not have to think about it at all. Consequently, when we wake up we *know* who we are, we *know* where we are, we *know* that we have to relieve ourselves, we *know* how to relieve ourselves, and we do so without having to consciously acknowledge it. We proceed throughout most of the rest of each day in a similar vein. In fact, we can get dressed, prepare our breakfast, get into and drive an automobile to work primarily by operating on a form of automatic pilot. In these instances such activities are a result of the workings of our prereflective consciousness. Of course, we may also use some deliberation or reflective thinking in choosing our particular behaviors.

When is it, then, that we actually do need to think? Given the fact that most of the time our prereflective consciousness *knows* what is going on and *knows* what we need to do, thinking would appear to be unnecessary through much of the day. Only at those times when we do not *know* as a prereflective consciousness do we need to use our will and engage in deliberate thinking. For example, in the morning we may believe that we need to make a list to organize ourselves so that we can efficiently complete all the necessary daily tasks. We compose lists because we trust or assume we will be more efficient with a written list of tasks.

When we address complex tasks, most of us assume that we need to use our reason, logic and deliberate thinking if we are to make good decisions and effectively solve problems. We have all been taught that humans are more highly developed than other species because of our ability to use language and to engage in rational thought. We hope that logic will solve all dilemmas, for it will guide us whenever the prereflective consciousness does not provide direction. Certainly, there are indeed times that rational thinking is very much called for and is necessary if we hope to be able to effectively problem solve. However, it is also possible that sometimes our search for logical solutions is not really the most rational choice but is, instead, a form of diversion or an exercise in self-deception.

Our prereflective consciousness is directed by the healthy side of the personality. Accordingly, we can basically trust that we will do the *right* and effective things without needing to engage in conscious thought. Although sometimes we may need high-powered logic as our guide, other times our prereflective consciousness might very well be telling us what we need to do. Often we do not trust that we are being pointed in the right direction. At such times the unhealthy side of the personality can then be the source of our self-doubt.

In other words, we may basically still *know* what is best to do, but our unhealthy side has placed seeds of doubt within us. I am proposing that we may very well *know* far more than we give ourselves credit for *knowing*. We might not need to have to engage in complex logical arguments because at certain times we indeed *know* what is the right choice to make. I am not suggesting that we can always know what is the right choice to make because we cannot be omniscient. However, we very well may *know* far more than we let ourselves believe that we know because of those strong interfering messages given by the unhealthy side of our personality.

We *know* things with different degrees of certainty. Sometimes we know very tentatively. At other times we are fairly sure of what we know. At still other times we feel certain of what we know. Still one further level of knowing I describe as *knowing in your bones*. What I mean by this is we can have an unshakable level of certainty beyond the knowing that is attained through logic. I am not speaking of the kind of certainty represented by our knowledge that the sun will come up tomorrow. Rather it is *knowing* what is the right choice for you to make or knowing what you must do with a level of conviction that cannot be compromised. It may be that you *know in your bones* that a particular person is the right individual for you to spend your life with. You may *know in your bones* what the right choice is in a given situation, despite what anyone else may say or believe.

This full and complete way of knowing I label *being plumb*. The dictionary offers several interesting definitions for the word "plumb." The particular meanings I want to convey with the word plumb are "to discover the facts of contents of; fathom, solve, understand" as well as the colloquial "entirely: wholly, absolutely"(*Webster's new world dictionary of the American language*, 1957). In colloquial language, we sometimes describe a person as being *plumb crazy*. One could also, theoretically, be *plumb healthy*. I believe that the road to becoming *plumb healthy* requires *being plumb* — being able to deeply know in ways that go beyond the presence of doubt. When you are *being plumb*, you know something so well that you would even be willing to stake your life on affirming this deep level of knowing. Many of us are familiar with using a plumb line to find what is the true center. Because walls in old houses often lean, it is necessary to know what is straight according to gravity. When we are plumb, we are centered and balanced in the universe.

When we are *being plumb,* our knowing is coming out of the healthy side of our personality. It is the full, deep level of knowing and acting that we see present in plants when they *know* to turn their leaves to avoid the rainstorm. It is the full, deep level of knowing that an animal possesses when it senses an approaching predator. It is the level of knowing in the dog who anticipates the master's impending heart attack. All of these actions or behaviors can also be accounted for by invoking biochemistry or theories of learning, but such explanations still cannot diminish the truth that all such activities are immediate, life-enhancing strategies used by many different life forms.

We can immediately know that the person we have just encountered will become a life-long friend or even a spouse. We can also profoundly know what is the right career choice for us and whether we should not accept a particular job. These forms of knowing are again examples of *being plumb*.

Because such levels of knowing are present in other life forms, we humans certainly must all possess the same capacity to know deeply and fully. However, all too often we have been trained to mistrust this deep level of knowing. Many people are even very skeptical that such a level of knowing exists. On the other hand, some of us very much want to possess that level of knowing despite the fact that we have not actually experienced such deep certainty. We can also deceive ourselves into believing that we fully know, or are *being plumb* when, in fact, we do not have that depth of knowing.

For example, I do not really see myself as clairvoyant yet there have been rare occasions in my life when I have *known* that a particular thing was going to happen and it then occurred. We have all heard about people whose *knowing* involves anticipating events with frightening regularity. However, *knowing* in the deep way is far broader and more important than occasionally *knowing* what the future will bring. When you really and fully *know* what to do in a crisis situation, you are *being plumb*. When you can say with conviction that you *know* what is right, you are *being plumb*. When you walk into a situation that does not feel right and you *know* you should immediately leave, you are *being plumb*.

At the times we can fully and deeply trust in ourselves and in our personal *knowing*, we are *being plumb*. Whenever we doubt ourselves and cannot hold onto what we know, the unhealthy side of our personality is in operation. The most basic truth is that at every moment we *know* a great deal, and usually we *know* far more than we credit ourselves. The times of self-doubt are the times when we lose *being plumb*.

Most of us have been repeatedly taught to mistrust what we know and instead to look outside ourselves for factual knowledge. As a result, it makes it extremely difficult for any individual to maintain the position *I fully and deeply know what is best now*. However, we need to remember that the words that spill out of our mouths and our actions are regularly and continually the immediate functions of our prereflective consciousness. Because virtually everything that we do comes out of our prereflective consciousness, we need to trust in the validity of prereflective consciousness. Because the prereflective consciousness utters coherent sentences and drives our automobiles and in so many ways immediately *knows* what to say and do, we can allow ourselves to appreciate this form of consciousness in far deeper ways. We can more and more often find ourselves *being plumb* when we trust our ability to *know* in the deepest ways.

We have all heard the advice that whenever we must make a difficult decision, we should "follow our gut." Such a suggestion implicitly recognizes the possibility of *being plumb,* for it affirms that we really *know* what is right because we have a basic and fundamental wisdom that can be our most trusted guide in life. All too often we humans assume the presence of definite limits to what we can actually *know*. I have come to realize, with age and experience, that there are fuller and deeper ways of *knowing* than I had previously considered. Such levels of *knowing* are not necessarily mystical, but they also cannot be accounted for by scientific investigation.

Nonetheless, *being plumb* cannot be a daily occurrence for it describes how one can feel and act only when important choices need to be made. We can trust ourselves functioning as prereflective consciousness and not need to reach for a higher level of knowing. I personally feel fairly certain of what I am about to do at any given moment, but this is not the level of certainty that is meant by *being plumb.* As a psychotherapist I trust that what I will say to my clients will be accurate and helpful, at least in the long run. However, there have been some occasions in which I *knew* that I had to take a very different form of intervention than I had ever previously taken. At those times I was *being plumb* because I deeply knew that this new strategy was the right course of action.

I described *being plumb* as *knowing in your bones.* In choosing that particular description I am conveying the truth that *being plumb* is more than simply a mental form of knowing. Rather, it is a total knowing that feels deeply right — a knowing that can be experienced bodily as well as mentally. Accordingly, when we are *being plumb*, we experience a state of exhilaration which combines a high level of self-confidence with a sense of participation in the world which is truly wondrous.

Whenever we must make difficult decisions and only look to logic for our guide, we can never find a level of certainly in our decision-making. Consequently, most existential writings state that we can never fully *know* what is right or what will prove to be the best course of action. I dispute that belief as being a universally valid description of the human condition. At those times that we are *being plumb*, we can deeply and fully know what is right, either for ourselves or for a situation. However, we are *being plumb* only a small proportion of the time.

Ideally, it would be wonderful if we regularly could be in a state of *being plumb* because we then would not feel doubt or dread. However, we all know that life is difficult with many occasions of uncertainty, pain and anguish. Because we all have been taught to engage in self-doubt and because we all have an unhealthy side to our personality, it is only on occasion that we are *being plumb*. Our goal is to reach for *being plumb* as much as possible and to trust in the truth that we all can and do *know* in very deep ways.

A general road map can direct us toward being plumb. The more we know ourselves, the more personal power we will own. The greater degree of personal power we feel, the more able we are to use our will to overcome our unhealthy tendencies. As our unhealthy side loses power, or to use the colloquialism *shrinks*, the more we can trust the knowing of our prereflective consciousness. The greater the reliance on the prereflective consciousness, the closer we come to the experience of *being plumb*. Finally, when we *know* what it is to *be plumb*, the more often we can trust and rely upon this feeling state to direct our choices.

Selfishness

Many people find it difficult to follow the healthy side of their personality. This problem may in part be due to the fact that during early childhood, the healthy sides were blocked or undermined by actions of their parents. Furthermore, one's healthy side is often devalued or undermined by the larger society or culture as well. Our social environment plays a crucial and influential role in our behavior, and society is primarily focused upon the preservation of itself rather than upon ensuring the gratification of any one member. As societal members we all are basically aware of and can effectively predict which behaviors will be rewarded, ignored or even punished by society at large. Because we can anticipate the possible reactions to our behavior, we know the importance of carefully choosing our actions. In that sense we all are very much affected by the societal network of social sanctions and rewards.

Even at those times when we decide to act in the face of social pressures, the struggle of making that decision demonstrates the widespread power of societal sanctions. We all have to find ways to satisfy our needs while living in a social context. Therefore, we need to consider the basic relationship existing between individuals and the larger society so that we can increase our level of personal power. Erich Fromm (1941) pointed out that society was initially created to satisfy the needs of the individual. Once that society became established, it developed its own needs which often conflicted with the particular needs of the individual. For example, the individual needs to stay alive, but often society demands that the citizen places his/her life in jeopardy by serving in the armed services.

The needs of a country are to win whatever war it becomes engaged in. As such, the country will draft many individuals into the armed services and is willing to allow many soldiers to die in order to serve the greater good of the society. To the degree that individuals are invested in nationalism and consider themselves to be good citizens, they become willing to sacrifice their personal lives for this supposedly greater good.

Societies are most effective when they convince individuals to subordinate their own personal needs to the larger societal needs. In the most effective forms of socialization, individuals specifically want to do what the larger society considers to be the most desirable actions. As another example, unattached individuals must pay taxes to support schools even though they themselves are childless. Their money could be spent paying for their own personal needs rather than for the needs of others, but good citizens make such sacrifices. Despite the fact that many countries are able to profoundly influence the individual to engage in self-sacrifice, Fromm acknowledges that no society has ever been able to provide for the full satisfaction of individual needs. Certainly, one's personal need is not to die prematurely, and yet there are times when many individuals do decide willingly to die for the preservation of the national ideals.

The larger society does allow for the general satisfaction of many individual needs, but it places limits on when, where and how an individual's needs are to be satisfied. Most people will feel good about themselves when they are able to satisfy their own needs by following the larger societal dictates. Because we humans are very social animals, we do need the approval and acceptance of others. However, there are times that we have unique wants. Our personal needs may then be in conflict with the needs of others or with the society at large.

When our personal desires conflict with the desires of other people, we have to choose whether to concede, compromise or simply proceed with satisfying our personal desires irrespective of the others' wishes. Making such choices is difficult because we not only face external pressures to compromise but also have internalized pressures to abandon our wishes and to serve the needs of others.

In both subtle and blatant ways we have been taught to subjugate our personal needs to societal needs. One form of influence is through language as we have a restricted number of available words to describe thoughts and feelings. If there are no words available to describe certain ways of thinking, we cannot effectively articulate certain kinds of thoughts. Consider the many instances in which you attempt to take care of yourself and satisfy your own needs. We do not have one word in English that describes such behavior in positive terms. The only word we do have to describe taking care of one's own personal needs is *selfish*. When considering the defined meaning of the word *selfish*, it is apparent that taking care of oneself is given a very negative connotation in the English language. Once again, because society wants the individual to subjugate personal needs to societal needs, it stands to reason that the individual who is satisfying personal needs may be looked upon with disfavor.

The primary need of society is to preserve and perpetuate itself while the primary need of the individual is self-preservation and enhancement. The needs of the individual are allowed to be gratified by the society at large provided that these behaviors do not interfere with the preservation of the society. It cannot be the major societal agenda for individuals simply to satisfy their own personal needs. Instead, the individual is expected to look beyond self and attend to the needs of others before focusing upon personal gratification. When the person simply attends to the satisfaction of personal needs, the society is not fundamentally satisfied. Certainly there are times when the satisfaction of personal needs is not in conflict with societal needs. But whenever the individual fails to think about the greater good, the society sees a potential risk present. Our society has taught us to label such behavior as selfish. Consequently, even when gratifying one's personal needs, one can be uneasy because the only word to use to describe the actions, *selfish*, has a negative connotation.

However, taking effective care of oneself and satisfying one's own needs is not a bad thing to do. It is absolutely necessary to look after yourself. If an individual does not attempt to gratify personal needs, it is most likely that those needs will not be satisfied. Once you are an adult, the only person who can and will take care of you is you. Such behavior is not self-indulgent but is self-preservative.

When people look to language to describe taking care of themselves in positive terms, they have to resort to the use of two words. The first word in such descriptions is usually "self." We say "self-indulgent," "self-protective," "self-affirming," "self-actualizing" – but none of these phrases has the proper connotation. Satisfying your basic and personal needs is a good and necessary action that is neither egotistic nor blind to the presence and/or needs of others.

Because we only have the word *selfish* to describe taking care of oneself, we are left with the strong implication that taking care of oneself will basically hurt someone else. Certainly, there are times when people are, in fact, selfish insofar as they attend to their own needs in ways that will deprive others or can even make them suffer. Such actions should not be condoned. However, if we make sure that we get a good job or lobby for a pay raise or buy a luxury item, these actions should not be described as selfish. But if buying that luxury item deprives others in your family of basic needs, then such actions can be described as selfish.

For effective and gratifying living it is necessary to recognize that we live in an interpersonal world and need to be attentive to the needs of those that we care about. We cannot be psychologically healthy and at the same time be fundamentally inconsiderate or oblivious to the needs of these others. Individuals who behave in such ways are considered narcissists. We primarily need to recognize the authenticity of our own needs and also recognize the validity of the needs of our significant others. Healthy humans, therefore, find a balance between being focused on the self and on the needs of others.

Irresolution between the need to satisfy self and the need to attend to others has been a human problem for centuries. The conflict over how and when we should act was perfectly described in the Talmud by Rabbi Hillel who asked

If I am not for myself who will be for me?
But when I am only for myself, what am I?
And if not now, when?

William James (1890) also made an interesting and indirect observation regarding selfishness. He said all human beings differ in a basic manner. We all divide the world into two parts—me and not me. Because all of us make such a division, James stated that no one could primarily be more interested in another person than they were in themselves. Nonetheless, our socialization process has placed great emphasis on attending to the needs of others. We must find ways to satisfy the needs of the people we love but not at any great loss to oneself.

Become alert if you ever hear someone begin a sentence with "If you really love me..." Such a statement demands deferring your own personal needs to satisfy the wishes of the other. We can meaningfully love another person on our terms and not on his/hers. When the other person starts to demand that we submit and accommodate to whatever they want, then the relationship stops being about love and becomes one of control.

Basically we can all either choose to please ourselves or choose to please another, and it is not inherently wrong or bad to please yourself. I recall that when I was in third grade, I was one of two candidates for class president. At the time of the vote I thought I was not supposed to vote for myself. I lost the election by one vote. I believe it highly likely that the other candidate did not share in my misguided perceptions, as I am sure he voted for himself. My actions at that time could be described as selfless, and *selfless* is a very interesting word that requires particular attention.

Acting in a selfless manner negates the basic truth that one has a self with needs. My vote in third grade denied myself and my own needs which, put simply, was stupid. If I had given enough credence to my needs, I would have been class president in third grade. Would that have made a difference in my life? I doubt it; but on the other hand I might not have become so engaged in the process of understanding myself and other people if I had regularly taken better care of myself as a child.

Life is best lived by not functioning at either end of the spectrum—i.e., by neither being primarily selfish nor primarily selfless. The key to effective living is both to be for oneself and also to recognize the importance of connections with others. It can be a tricky balancing act. Nonetheless, making difficult choices is one activity which makes our lives most rewarding. When we struggle over difficult choices, we often wish that we just *knew* what was best to do. However, once we have made the choice and it has worked out well, we can feel justly proud of our decision-making. Choosing is central to our existence and, therefore, requires further discussion.

On Responsibility

At birth we begin to learn how to have our needs satisfied. Our bodies demand that we breathe, eat and eliminate bodily waste. Although we initially engage in these activities because they are instinctively driven, we soon can alter and regulate eating, elimination and even to some degree breathing through the process of learning. It does not take the infant very long to learn that crying brings people closer and that people provide need satisfaction. Crying, a natural biological activity, soon becomes a useful technique the child uses to demand food, care and attention. The infant and small child cry not only to have their biological needs met but also to demand physical contact and warmth from the adult. At the very outset of the infant's life, adults are usually quite willing to satisfy all of the infant's desires. Yet it does not take very long for parental figures to develop some expectations of the child.

These expectations can be described as a major component in the process of socializing children. Adults teach children how to make sense of the world by identifying different objects and by distinguishing between what is safe and what is dangerous. Parents also will intervene in varying degrees at different ages sometimes to stop and even scold the child for engaging in what is considered unacceptable or dangerous behavior. The child is taught not to bite the parent, not to hit others, how to use the toilet, etc. In other words, the child learns which are the appropriate behaviors and which are not.

Children learn what parents basically want them to do for several different reasons. Sometimes, children conform and comply with parental wishes because they have learned that pleasing parents produces rewards. Furthermore, because of the emotional bond with parents it feels good for the child, in and of itself, to behave in ways that generate greater interpersonal closeness. Of course, often there is conflict between what the child wants to do at any given moment and what the parent wants the child to do. For example, when a young child feels the urge to urinate, the child is likely to do so immediately; the parent much prefers that the child use the potty. It takes a long time for the young child to learn to defer and delay certain behavior patterns in order to please the parental figures.

It is basic to the parental role to teach the child how to function effectively in the world, and that process requires much patience and understanding. The capable parent teaches the child how best to understand and get along well with other people. The child is told what behaviors are appropriate and what behaviors are unacceptable. Furthermore, parents demand more complex and sophisticated behaviors as their children continue to mature.

Parents also begin to teach the child certain responsibilities they are to carry out. For example, the child may be asked to put away toys before going to bed or to monitor the behavior of a younger sibling. As children mature, their responsibilities increase. Many parents believe the child's primary responsibility is to perform well at school. Others may consider it mandatory for the child to assume different familial tasks, i.e., work in the yard, help with the dishes, etc. Effective parents develop reasonable expectations for their children and revise these expectations as children become older.

Fulfilling such responsibilities often is a source of personal pride for the child. At other times, these responsibilities may be seen as onerous tasks. As a result, sometimes the child will enjoy behaving responsibly while at other times the child may resent or even hate these demands.

Along with teaching children appropriate behaviors and basic responsibilities parents also distinguish what behaviors are *right* as opposed to what are *wrong*. Parents not only specify bad behaviors, but also they may label certain kinds of thoughts as bad or even shameful. Such teaching represents the beginning steps of a moral education which leads to the development of a conscience in a child.

To reiterate, most children learn 1) what to do in order to get their needs met; 2) what are the appropriate behaviors to engage in; 3) what are their responsibilities; and 4) what are the right and wrong things to do. These expectations are not experienced by children as being separate and discrete tasks. Rather, they are felt as "all of a piece." In other words, there is a large package of expectations children know they are supposed to follow.

Because children, just like adults, are not primarily interested in satisfying the needs of other people, we can anticipate that children will not always do what parents desire. Nonetheless, because parents have the most power in managing the family and in dispensing rewards and punishments, it is common for children primarily to conform to the parents' wishes and expectations.

Erich Fromm (1955) pointed out that societies are effective when they make individuals believe they are willingly behaving in the ways society wants them to act. Parents socialize their children in such a manner. They teach children to engage in appropriate activities, which are the socially desired behaviors. Thereby, the parents function as the agents of the larger subgroup or society.

Even though pre-adolescent children will often balk, rebel or defy parental expectations, such resistance is usually insignificant compared to the much larger rebellion likely to occur during adolescence. The basic task of adolescence is to move toward independence—in other words, to become one's own person. Such personal development involves thinking for oneself and primarily acting independently of the wishes of others. However, the first steps toward developing one's own personal viewpoint will usually involve rejecting most of the parental rules and expectations. Therefore, it is quite common for the adolescent to be defiant and to rebel, seemingly for the sake of rebelling. The adolescent will often say "no" with the same kind of emphatic stubborn stance previously seen in a two-year-old.

Adolescents can rebel against all four of the parental dictates previously mentioned. That is, they can refuse to follow the problem-solving strategies that parents endorsed. They can and do rebel against engaging in what their parents considered to be appropriate behavior patterns. They can refuse to follow the moral code endorsed by the parent. Furthermore, it is very common for adolescents to refuse to fulfill the responsibilities placed upon them by their parents.

Because during childhood responsibility is often viewed as a series of externally imposed demands, it is inevitable that upon reaching adolescence teenagers no longer want to fulfill these responsibilities. They do not want to be continually accountable to someone else for their behavior. The most fervent wish of adolescents is to be free and, most particularly, they define freedom as *freedom from responsibility* (Frankl, 1960). This is a very natural and healthy wish for it is a stage that we all need to pass through. We can develop true independence only if we are seriously willing to question the validity of all the many rules, expectations and responsibilities that we have been taught.

Being able to say "no" to virtually all external expectations can feel liberating, at least for a period of time.

However, as Frankl points out, simply saying "no" does not help the person decide what to do. We all will regularly need to pose the question to ourselves, *What should I do and when should I do it?*

When we ask such questions, we implicitly accept the important truth that each of us is capable of choosing what to do and what not to do. For Frankl, we thereby pass through the stage of considering freedom to represent *freedom from responsibility* into understanding that what we actually possess is the *freedom to be* (personally) *responsible.* In accepting the truth that we are constantly making choices out of our own free will, we begin to recognize we alone are responsible for all the big and little choices that we make. Responsibility then acquires a very different meaning because it refers to what we owe to ourselves rather than representing what we owe to other people.

All of us struggle to some degree with this problem of responsibility. When we think about having free choice, we want to be able to choose desirable or pleasant alternatives. Many times, however, we must choose among undesirable possibilities, such as who cleans the toilet and who washes the kitchen floor. Certain life situations demand that we make particularly painful choices and because of the anguish we feel at those times, many of us fail to admit that we have the free will to make a choice. Too often freedom is viewed as representing freedom from being responsible rather than as freedom to be responsible. When we do not own the truth that we ourselves made a difficult choice, we prevent ourselves from feeling the pride that accompanies responsible adult decisions.

Our interpersonal environment requires us to regularly deal with the expectations and demands of others. We all are well aware of the many things we have to do and for which we are responsible. As college students we are expected to attend classes, comply with assignments and submit to examinations. If we fail to complete these requirements in a satisfactory manner, we receive a failing grade in the course. Students have an implicit contract with the teacher: students are expected to satisfy the course requirements, and the teacher is expected to evaluate them fairly on their performance. In academic situations students have a responsibility to fulfill that implicit contract. But to whom is the student actually responsible?

The college student is not responsible to the professor, as the instructor does not basically care whether the student satisfies the course requirements. The student will simply be graded on level of performance. If professors are invested in wanting the students to learn the material, the professors will be unhappy with a poor performance. Nonetheless, it is not the teacher's responsibility to make the student learn or perform well.

The implicit student-professor contract becomes a model for the implicit contract that takes place in the work environment. The employee is expected to perform specific jobs. If the job duties are performed well, the employee will be rewarded financially, either by keeping the job or by receiving a raise. If the employee fails to carry out the job responsibilities, the employee will likely be fired. However, here, too, the question remains, to whom is the employee responsible?

Because the quality of one's performance does not essentially matter to the professor or the employer, i.e., you can receive a failing grade or be fired and be replaced by someone else, we must look elsewhere to find where the obligations lie. It may be that students feel responsible to their parents for performing well in school. If the parents pay for a college education, they certainly are entitled to specify what they are willing to pay for and what they expect in return. The student has the choice of either accepting or rejecting those terms, and the student will most likely face different consequences for either fulfilling or failing to fulfill these expectations.

Nonetheless, students cannot be responsible primarily to parents for their academic performance. When deciding to attend college, students are informed of the required standards in order to maintain a matriculated status. In making the choice to attend college, just as with all other choices, the individual is then primarily responsible for having made that choice. Others may hold the individual accountable for a poor performance, but they cannot be the main or even valid judges of the individual's actions. Because you are freely making choices, even when they are difficult choices, you must still answer to yourself for your actions.

Correspondingly, at the job site, the employee can attempt to rationalize and blame the boss for being too tough or rigid; but it is difficult to sustain blaming others for our own inadequate performance. We are each responsible to ourselves for how we function, irrespective of the actions of the other person.

We ourselves choose what to do in different situations, and we know that there will ultimately be consequences for our choices. In realizing that we choose how to live our lives, we are then personally responsible for our choices. We are primarily responsible to ourselves. Being accountable to oneself is far more difficult and troublesome than being accountable to another. We can always try to manipulate, deceive or even blame another person in order to not accept the responsibility for our actions. It becomes far more difficult, if not impossible, to make effective excuses to ourselves for our faulty actions.

It is difficult, painful and awesome to accept the truth that it is we ourselves who have the power to direct the course of our lives. Knowing we are the choosers means that we will be inescapably responsible for our choices. It is not difficult to be responsible for our lives at specific times, especially when we are facing easy choices. However, to be responsible all the time is truly humbling. Realizing our power and responsibility can be both empowering and potentially terrifying.

We humans gladly take responsibility when we are fairly certain what the right choices are. We would prefer not to be responsible when we have to make ugly choices. To choose between death by hanging or death by drowning does not feel like much of a choice. However, we often must make choices between two undesirable alternatives. Not only do we hate having to face such alternatives before us but we also do not want to assume the responsibility of making such choices.

Furthermore, the adolescent remains alive in all of us. Consequently, at times we view responsibilities as externally imposed demands rather than as possibilities for self-assertion and pride. In those instances we may feel oppressed, resentful and without power. We may then refuse to carry out these responsibilities, and we revert to more childlike behavior patterns.

Such is the problem with responsibility. We relish responsibility when we are self-assured, but we want to relinquish responsibility when we must make difficult decisions or have to complete onerous tasks. Nonetheless, we are the only ones who can legitimately be considered responsible for the choices we make.

Even when you are manipulated into a problematic situation, you are ultimately responsible for having allowed yourself to have been so manipulated. Whatever predicaments you face, you yourself must find a way to resolve the situation. Blaming and being angry with others for manipulation never solves the problem at hand.

People who see themselves as victims can turn that knowledge into positive uses. One of my therapy patients stated that he was a psychological wreck because of the cruel ways he had been treated by both of his parents. He initially resented that it was his job to make himself healthier. However, he came to realize that only he alone could fix the scars created by this unjust treatment. So it is, too, for all of us. In some ways we each have been victimized, and we are still responsible for repairing ourselves as other human beings cannot heal us.

It is an unfortunate situation when we have to be responsible for either choosing to repair our lives or to live in anguish. In order to avoid the pain of making difficult decisions and then carrying the responsibility for such decisions, we may tell ourselves that we are incapable of making significant choices. We may say either that others hold power over us or that we are inadequate and therefore unable to make important decisions. We deny having the power to make choices because we do not want to assume the responsibility of having made those choices. This attempt to avoid personal responsibility only produces additional pain. To believe that you cannot act is to lie to yourself and believe you are much weaker than you actually are. Furthermore, you face more pain when you realize that you are just as responsible for deciding *not* to make a choice as you are whenever you do make a choice. As Sartre (1943) said, there is *No exit* from this difficult human condition.

Even when we are willing to accept responsibility for our choices, we can still create major pain for ourselves. When you evaluate your recent choices and actions, it is possible for your unhealthy side to assume the role of primary judge. When this occurs, even though you may believe you are engaged in the process of rational self-evaluation, you are really being tyrannized by your unhealthy side. Furthermore, the attack takes place simply because once again it is being demonstrated that you are a fallible human being.

We can and certainly will make some wrong choices in our lives, but poor choices do not at all justify ongoing and vitriolic self-blame. We are all able to recognize our mistakes after they occur, and we usually can learn from them. We are able to forgive ourselves for our errors and will move forward with our lives whenever the healthy side of our personality is in control. However, if the unhealthy side makes the evaluations, we will be subject to continual self-attack.

To summarize, we do have freedom to make choices and, consequently, we are ultimately responsible for our actions. However, the emotion of anxiety plays an ongoing role in much of our decision making. Recognizing that we make choices can cause anxiety. We are anxious because we want to make the right choices but simultaneously recognize we can very well make the wrong choices. That implicit recognition of our fallibility creates our anxiety, and it is enormously difficult for us to accept that being human means being deficient.

Making Choices

All of our actions serve particular purposes. We engage in certain behavior patterns because we have certain intentions. Although our actions are designed to satisfy our intentions, few of these intentions are deliberately thought out. For example, at times we find ourselves opening the refrigerator door. It seems quite likely our intention was to eat and, consequently, we walked to the refrigerator and opened the door, seemingly automatically. There was a purpose to our behavior, and it was carried out quickly without particular deliberation. We are also all aware that there are times when we say "I am hungry" and then walk to the refrigerator. At other times, we have opened the refrigerator door without even recognizing we were thinking about food.

It is not very difficult to recognize the purposes behind our behaviors because we, as very efficient creatures, usually have a very direct link between our intentions and our subsequent behavior. However, in order to be even more efficient and successful, we need to study our behavior patterns to detect whether the healthy or unhealthy side of the personality has directed our actions.

We want to reach or accomplish certain goals and, therefore, we do specific things we believe will lead us to those goals. In that sense we are constantly making choices which reflect our underlying intentions. Some of the time we do make these choices quite deliberately. At other times, the choices are made through prereflective consciousness. Nonetheless, we ourselves must have made these choices because we are the agents propelling ourselves into activities. Opening the refrigerator door must always be considered a choice, even when it appears to be automatic.

Some choices are made in the absence of deliberate or conscious choice for a number of reasons. At some times it may be more efficient to act without keeping the goal in the forefront of our minds. For example, if students keep focusing for an A on a test, rumination over whether they can ace the exam could well interfere with the act of studying. It would, therefore, be more efficient not to deliberately focus upon the need to excel but rather to simply do what needs to be done.

At other times inner conflicts may play out in our behavior before we realize a struggle is actually taking place. For example, a concern with overweight might lead to a decision not to eat any more snack foods. Yet, this person might very well still feel hungry. As a result, the hungry part leads the individual to the refrigerator in an attempt to deceive the part which wishes to diet. When such a scenario is played out, you must own up to the fact that you have indeed chosen to eat. We also need to acknowledge that the dieter represents the healthy part, and snacking is an expression of the unhealthy part. The behavior was of one part deceiving another part. Choices still produce our behaviors even when they appear to be made without deliberate awareness.

Minute-by-minute we are making choices. We make ourselves sit down or stand up. We choose to work, to talk or to sleep. We enter into problem-solving activities, and at other times we decide to relax by turning on electronic equipment. All of our actions result from the implicit or explicit choices we make. We can choose to be actively aware of the choices that stand before us, or we may choose to continue to function on a form of automatic pilot. When we plod along in life without deliberately engaging in much contemplation or reflection, that, too, is a choice. However, the automatic pilot mode is not always efficient and helpful. At times this form of automatic behaving can keep us from being aware of the available positive choices we can make. At such times we are *not thinking* because the unhealthy side of our personality has stopped us from being able to move forward.

Sometimes our choices produce very significant changes in our lives. Through such choices we can shape and even recreate ourselves. On the other hand, we can also continue to make the same choices, day after day and week after week, and in that manner we may prevent ourselves from growth and change. It is through our choices that we establish, maintain or begin to change the course of our lives.

In order to make the most effective choices, we must first recognize exactly what we want. Once we know our wishes, we can create and implement a plan of action. The plan can be as simple as opening the refrigerator door, which could be done without deliberate thinking. Nonetheless, opening the refrigerator is the choice that we made. We are the agents who choose what to do and what not to do, sometimes with our eyes fully open and sometimes with our eyes fully closed.

Most of the decisions or choices that we make on a daily basis can be described as little choices. We are continually making these little choices virtually every moment of the day. We first decide whether to push the snooze button on the alarm clock or simply get out of bed. We decide what to wear, what to eat for breakfast, which part of the newspaper to read; and we continue to make similar decisions on a moment-to-moment basis as we proceed through each day. These are examples of the insignificant choices which rarely will have long-term effects on our lives. However, sometimes one of these small and seemingly unimportant choices can turn out to have major consequences in our lives.

If we were to focus on the possibility that each little choice might profoundly alter our lives, we would probably become immobilized. If you believe that every little thing you do can transform your life, you will become excessively cautious and ultimately unable to make even simple decisions. We cannot ponder over every small choice because first of all, it is far too time-consuming. Furthermore, decision-making would become overwhelming if we give excessive meaning to each possible choice. As a result, we make many of our daily choices automatically.

Most of the time we do not let ourselves realize that the little choices we make are actually choices at all. Rather, our actions can become robotic. We pick the blue blouse instead of the white blouse. We keep the alarm clock set at the same time each morning. We make the breakfast coffee without deliberate thought. In other words, many choices we make on a daily basis do not appear to be the result of any actual decision-making process.

Many of us avoid acknowledgment of our routinely made little choices. Such people say "I have to be in class or in school at such and such a time" or "I have to shop... cook...be nice...or call my parents." When you tell yourself you have to do a particular activity instead of accepting the truth that you are choosing to do it, you deceive yourself into believing that you do not have power even though you are the person who makes the event occur.

Consider what happens when garbage accumulates in your kitchen. Many of us will say to ourselves that we *must* take out the garbage. When we speak to ourselves in such a manner, we consider ourselves controlled by external demands. We do not really want to get up from our comfortable position and take out the garbage. We have better things to do with our time. To say "I have to" or "I must" implies we have no choice in the matter. However, we could choose to leave the rotting garbage in the kitchen and tolerate the odor as it increases. We do not really have to remove garbage. Few people are willing to live with the odor, and so we remove the garbage from the house.

Most of us do not consider garbage removal to be a free choice but rather view it as a necessary activity. Many of the other choices we make are also necessary choices. We need to have money in order to pay our bills so we *must* go to work. Again, it is too impractical and problematic just to choose the most pleasurable activity. Rather, we must choose among alternatives that often are not always pleasant. However, if we deceive ourselves into believing that the decisions we made were what we *had to do*, then we change our self-image and see ourselves as victims. Whenever we see ourselves as having to conform to external demands, we can soon feel manipulated and angry at these outside forces. On the other hand, some of us may stifle the desire to rebel because of our perceived powerlessness, and force ourselves to do "the right thing." By such mental gymnastics we both lost our sense of personal power and simultaneously established stricter control over our desires. We also take away our sense of responsibility for our actions, but that issue will be discussed later.

When one considers not conforming to external expectations, such as the college student who wants to cut classes or the worker who ponders calling in sick, the person is always free to make such choices. Of course, there very well may be consequences of being absent or being present. All choices have potential consequences, an unpleasant fact especially when we have to choose among undesirable possibilities. It is a fond but unrealistic wish to be able to rebel against expected behavior and then not have the defiance produce negative consequences. Unfortunately, meaningful choices can and do have consequences. Otherwise they would not really be choices.

Deciding whether or not to take a sick day from work or school is one example of what I call a little decision. In contrast, there are "big" choices to be made that are likely to have lasting consequences. These big decisions include topics such as "What kind of career do I want?"; "With whom do I want to live?"; and "Where do I want to spend my life?" It is pointless to make an exhaustive list of what are the little and what are the big choices as most of us immediately can sense and distinguish among them.

The little choices are easy to make because we believe they will not have significant consequences. Because we recognize that the big decisions can have major consequences, we find these choices more difficult. At times we may become so afraid of potential consequences that we engage in a major form of self-deception rather than choose. We tell ourselves we are not capable of making a choice, or we are trapped and powerless. In fact, we are afraid to make the choices that could set us free of the trap.

When we have to make big choices, at times it feels extremely difficult and sometimes even impossible to decide what is the better choice. All of us remember different occasions, agonizing over particular choices. Of course, at other times making a difficult choice has been very easy. Those are the occasions when we are *being plumb*. Most of us wish we could always fully know the better choice to make, finding ourselves *being plumb* as we proceed in life.

In my work as a therapist I have often heard unhappily married people say that they were unable to leave their spouses. When asked to explain why, they made statements such as divorce is too costly, both financially and/or emotionally. The implicit reason for inaction is they did not want to face the negative consequences of making such difficult choices. Explicitly it becomes easier to say that they do not really have a choice rather than admit they have the power to take difficult or problematic action.

A major psychotherapist, Viktor Frankl (1960), believed that whenever we accepted the inevitability of our own mortality, we would become much more able to make difficult choices. He stated that knowing we are all going to die places an urgency upon the moment. If our lives were eternal, we would have all the time in the world to make our choices and all of our actions could be delayed or repaired. Mistakes could all be redone in the next 20, 50 or 500 years. Because human existence is limited in time, Frankl believed we must make our time and our choices count. Consequently, we need to see that we do have the power and capacity to make meaningful choices; and it is imperative not to needlessly delay taking action.

Nonetheless, we face a difficult dilemma. On the one hand, too much thinking about potential consequences of choices will render us immobile; on the other hand, refusing to acknowledge that our choices will have consequences can lead to impulsive and irresponsible actions. We have to find a balance — between recognizing that we have the power to make important choices while simultaneously relaxing internal pressures so we can make important decisions based upon our best instincts and knowledge.

Life might seem much easier if we were simply unaware that we had the capacity to make meaningful choices. Blissful ignorance sounds free of pain. Unfortunately, when we do not keep our eyes open, we are likely to walk into major trouble. We need to maintain an awareness of ourselves and situations even though such knowledge, at times, can be uncomfortable. If you had to walk across a busy intersection at night with your eyes either open or closed, which would you choose?

Making choices is both frightening and empowering, and we need to be aware of both feelings. Individuals with a strong healthy side can use choices to feel even more empowered. Nonetheless, even for the healthy person it is still very important to know the unhealthy side can intervene. We must all guard against that possibility by developing enough self-awareness to insure the healthy side is in control. Vigilance is necessary for everyone, and it is most important for those with a powerful unhealthy side.

Additional powerful components involved in making healthy choices are responsibility and anxiety. Whenever we make "big" or important choices, anxiety is always involved. Such anxiety is healthy although a very uncomfortable experience. Because we are the sole agents choosing, we are, inescapably, personally responsible for these choices.

Understanding Anxiety

No one wants to feel the discomfort of anxiety. It varies in intensity as it can be experienced as a mild sense of unease which can accelerate into a state of sheer panic similar to immobilized terror. Several different words have been used to describe this state of inner turmoil. Today the word "stress" is more frequently used than the term anxiety. When people say they are under stress, they imply the reason for their discomfort is an external event, such as a demanding job or a difficult child. However, often our discomfort is essentially created by ourselves. Therefore, anxiety is a better descriptive word to use than stress for it does not imply what has caused this state of discomfort. Dread is an even better description than anxiety. Dread conjures up feelings of unease more readily than do either the words anxiety or stress. Irrespective of which word is preferred, most people strongly wish and hope they will never have to re-experience these negative feelings.

Because so many individuals suffer from frequent periods of anxiety, it is not surprising that a host of different procedures and techniques have been devised to help people become calmer. In fact, psychotherapy was initially created in order to alleviate the crippling anxiety that had been destroying peoples' lives. Psychotherapists now treat a fuller range of human problems in addition to anxiety, but it is the personal discomfort of anxiety that remains the prime motivation for individuals to seek psychotherapeutic assistance. Many people today prefer to use anti-anxiety medication to reduce their discomfort, and they consult physicians and psychiatrists for such prescriptions. Others attempt to self-medicate their anxiety by taking illegal drugs or alcohol. Still others try to treat their anxiety independently by reading self-help books, practicing meditation and listening to relaxation tapes, attending workshops or getting frequent massages. Many different methods are available to decrease anxiety, all of which have varying degrees of success.

A multitude of strategies has been devised to alleviate anxiety because millions of people do experience major stress and inner turmoil. However, some forms of anxiety are not destructive to human functioning but, in fact, can be helpful survival techniques. Psychologists have demonstrated through many research studies that people perform at an optimum level when experiencing a moderate degree of anxiety. On the other hand, both very high and very low anxiety levels lead to less efficient performance.

Rollo May (1977) explained that anxiety is a necessary and routine part of living by distinguishing between what he labeled normal and neurotic anxiety. He believed it was natural or normal for people to feel some anxiety whenever they faced life's difficulties. We all encounter events and situations which are scary, and feeling anxious at those times is indeed perfectly normal and expected.

However, some individuals refuse to admit they are "weak enough" to be anxious, and they try to keep anxious feelings outside of their experiential world. May (1977) explained that such attempts to block anxiety will typically fail, if not in the immediate moment then certainly later in time. He believed this underlying anxiety would ultimately break into one's awareness in an unpredictable and therefore irrational manner. When anxiety appears in this disruptive and irrational way, it is considered to be neurotic anxiety. People who experience such dread do not know why they are so uncomfortable. But according to May, they experience neurotic anxiety because they did not allow themselves to experience normal anxiety.

Normal anxiety is typically felt whenever we know that something important can likely affect us in an adverse fashion. We do not feel anxious as a result of performing everyday activities such as tying shoelaces or taking out the garbage. Normal anxiety is experienced in meaningful situations which can have important consequences. Based upon what we do in those important situations, we either have a sense of triumph or a sense of loss. We interpret these situations as having high significance, and we implicitly know that our action or lack of action can and will effect the ultimate outcome. For example, whenever we meet someone we find attractive and want to impress, we are all likely to experience normal anxiety. We want the other person to find us attractive, but we worry (are anxious) about what we can do to make us seem especially desirable and appealing. Our anxiety becomes activated because we want to make a good impression but remain uncertain as to which behavior will best serve that goal.

This simple example demonstrates why anxiety, choice and responsibility are so closely interrelated. Once we recognize a particular wish and want it to come true, i.e., we want to appear attractive to a particular other person, we then experience anxiety. The anxiety is a consequence of our realization that we have a choice as to how to act and how not to act. When you want to make a good impression, you must first select from the wide variety of different possible behavior patterns at your disposal. You feel anxious because you want to choose the most effective behavior, but you cannot be sure as to what will work and what will fail. You recognize that you alone must choose what to do and therefore you implicitly know you are responsible for the success or failure of the chosen behaviors. You become anxious because you have to make a meaningful choice and must bear the responsibility for that choice. In other words, you can make either the right or the wrong choices, and you will reap the benefits or suffer the consequences of these choices.

It is highly unlikely for us to experience anxiety whenever we are choosing between alternatives which seem to hold no special meaning. Whether you wear the blue shirt or the green shirt does not typically cause anxiety. However, one might even give that choice excessive meaning and agonize over whether the shirt color will produce success or failure. It stands to reason that if we give inordinate meaning to many small choices, we will ultimately become immobilized with anxiety.

If we do not attribute excessive meaning to our choices, then anxiety will not be experienced on a regular basis. It is our personal interpretation of what is or is not at stake that will either make us anxious or keep us relaxed. I do not mean to imply there are no significant threats in our world. Rather, what I am suggesting is that we each individually create the particular degree of threat we experience. Examine more closely the example of wanting to make a positive impression on another.

Individuals vary enormously in terms of how important they think it is to be seen in a favorable light. Some of us are willing to accept the fact that others may not find us attractive; and if we fail to impress a particular person, we simply look elsewhere for validation. Others cannot be so casual if a particular person shows no interest in them. Some individuals routinely anticipate rejection, believing themselves to be undesirable people. Because of these negative feelings, they may not even have acquired behavioral techniques to make them appear more appealing. Consequently, their method of approach will most likely produce rejection and thereby reaffirm an already low level of self-esteem. Others may even feel so much threat over potential rejection that they never initiate a move toward the other person.

Certainly no one ever has full control over whether another person will respond positively. Some people are unable to accept this basic truth. They make it imperative to *always* impress, disregarding the fact that the other person may have personal preferences or already be involved in a committed relationship. By disregarding such possibilities, these individuals may launch into self-blame whenever they fail to impress. It is relatively easy to see how the unhealthy side of the person has taken control of feelings in such situations.

The more we mistakenly believe we have full power to affect others, the more likely it is for us to be subjected to anxiety. The more we demand that we be successful, the greater the possibility that we can fail. Because of this high possibility of failure when we make excessive demands on ourselves, anxiety is likely to appear *before* any action is taken. On the other hand, if our internal demands are reasonable, then we will experience a more moderate level of anxiety. In either case the anxiety serves as a warning signal about important choices. When we have unrealistic expectations, our anxiety will become too intense, thereby blocking us from taking effective action.

Anxiety is, therefore, quite a complicated emotion. If it is experienced at a low to moderate level, one can then be warned and be able to exercise good judgment in making effective choices. If the anxiety accelerates too much, the person will feel too immobilized for action and could be subject to an anxiety attack. A person's anxiety is most likely to intensify when it is connected to unreasonable demands that cannot be satisfied.

When we have a mild degree of anxiety, we sense our ability to do something immediately to avoid trouble. For example, most of us feel anxious before making a public presentation. We feel anxious because we know there could be important consequences from a poor presentation. The anxiety alerts us to the need to prepare well in order to excel. Without any performance anxiety, we will not feel an urgency about advance preparation and probably will not make a good showing. Anxiety is first and foremost a helpful warning, and we need this warning to mobilize our resources.

Unfortunately, we are not always able to heed the warnings from anxiety. When we do not take effective action to deal with what may be an important situation, our anxiety will immobilize us. At other times we may try to avoid anxious feelings through the distraction of other activities. The problem with distractions is that they provide only temporary relief; ultimately we must deal with the uncomfortable situation.

We feel anxious because we have potential power to control the outcome of an important situation. If we had no sense of potential power to succeed in troubling situations, we would not feel anxious. Instead, we would feel depressed. This distinction is the major difference between anxiety and depression. When people feel anxious, they sense their potential power; and when they feel depressed, they sense they are simply powerless. However, it is also possible to feel both anxiety and depression, both potential power and powerlessness.

To take responsible action when you are anxious not only eliminates your anxiety but also make you feel exhilarated. Your greatest sense of triumph occurs when you have taken positive action in the face of anxious feelings. Some of the proudest moments of our lives are when we have refused to back down, despite feeling intimidated and potentially overwhelmed. Theoretically the same sense of triumph could occur if one were able to take positive action in the face of depression. Unfortunately, depression saps motivation and any sense of power. Consequently in the moment, the depressed person does not believe it possible to take effective action. Under such conditions the depression is likely to increase in intensity, causing even more immobility.

Because anxiety can increase in intensity whenever we fail to take action, the best strategy is to take action quickly. Even though facing anxiety is difficult, it is by far the best way to reduce its strength. The longer you wait to take action when you are anxious, the more intense the anxiety becomes. This escalation of anxiety represents the actions of the unhealthy side of the personality. We need to trust ourselves that we can and will choose effective courses of action despite the anxiety and then use this trust to move forward. Even if our judgment proves wrong, we can still take comfort that we have given the situation our "best shot." Because full confidence of success at all times is not possible, we will feel anxious at different times.

To take action when feeling anxious requires courage and strength of character, described by Paul Tillich (1952) in his book *The Courage to Be*. When we do act under such circumstances, not only do we become proud of these actions but also we move our lives forward. When we act in spite of feeling anxious, we are, in fact, creating ourselves by choosing a different way of feeling and being. It is more accurate to say we take ourselves to a higher level of functioning. It is through the use of our will to move forward that we reach new heights of being. By such actions we make changes in ourselves; by engaging in such actions, we implicitly affirm our inherent power to shape and change our lives.

It is indeed awesome that we can move away from the dread of anxiety by affirming our will in a manner that produces our greatest triumphs. What we accomplish at such moments is a triumph over our unhealthy side, the best outcome for situations in which we experience anxiety. We can feel proud because we have taken constructive action in the face of much discomfort and dread. It is when we know we must move forward, despite anxiety and tension, and make difficult decisions in the light of much uncertainty that we humans become most admirable and heroic. We would like to eliminate pain; but if all pain were to disappear, courage would be neither needed nor exhibited.

It is ironic that we can move from the dreadful feelings of anxiety to the triumphant feelings of conquering our unhealthy side. One of the greatest insights of the existential thinkers is that one always has an opposite alternative to consider. We can only understand fear because we have experienced security. If we felt anxiety all the time, it would soon be an insignificant experience. It is only because at times we have the opposite feeling that we can know the full import of any feeling. In dialectic reasoning we can fully grasp pleasure because we know what it is to experience pain. We fully know what it is to love because we know what it is to hate. Most of us remember how in times of sickness we particularly appreciate what it was like when we had full physical health. Although we may vow to appreciate our physical health once it fully returns, too often we forget and take good health for granted.

To review the complex interconnection of our experiences, we are anxious because we must act or make meaningful choices. We are responsible to ourselves for the choices that we make. However, we cannot know most of the time that our choices will be correct. Sometimes, we are *being plumb* and can *know* what is the right thing to do and then do it. Most of the time, however, we must act with uncertainty. Such is the human condition.

ANXIETY AND CHANGE

Whenever we experience anxiety, we are hearing a call to action. To deal effectively with the anxiety means to be willing to do something different. In order to live a healthy and fulfilling life it is necessary to embrace change. Even as important as it is to allow change, it is also just as necessary at times to refuse change. In other words, we need to establish a comfortable balance between remaining basically the same person and transforming into a new and different person. Continual change would cause a kind of free fall where we could not draw upon any of the knowledge gained from the past. If such a condition were to happen, we would become disoriented and unable to make any sense of the immediate moment.

It is quite common in adolescence to go through a phase of trying on different identities over short periods of time. The teenager shifts from being a *femme fatale* to renouncing sex, from being a serious student to having a carefree, devil-may-care attitude. For the teenager, these radical shifts come and go quite quickly. For adults, such lightening fast changes prove too disorienting. To change at an even faster pace would be terrifying.

Yet if we do not allow ourselves ever to change, we become rigid and unwilling to learn or profit from our experiences. Such inflexibility would keep us from successfully adapting to new life situations for we would basically be acting the same at age 53 as we did at age 13. It is an arduous but vitally important task to find an effective balance between maintaining an openness to change while holding on to central aspects of our beliefs and personal identity.

Most existential writers tell us that each moment is unique and consequently, we are all new in the moment. This view is more theoretically true than it can be experientially true. If every moment were totally new, we could not make sense of the situation. We all need a sense of continuity from moment to moment. We need to have language, a sense of self and a basic way of understanding our surroundings. It is impossible and intolerable to experience life as incessantly changing. On the other hand, every moment cannot be the same as the previous moment because otherwise we would never change, grow or develop. Each moment is, in fact, unique while concomitantly similar to previous moments. Again, we need to balance the two perspectives.

We are creatures both who change and who do not change. The changes can be large or small, and at some times we do not change at all. One of the most helpful concepts for understanding other people is to assess their openness to change. People can close off all possibilities of change or they can allow for a multitude of changes in themselves. For example, one may say *Today is the same old Monday where I go to the same job and follow the same routine from morning till night.* On the other hand, one can approach each day as a potentially important new experience with new information, new perspectives and new adventures. We would not be very credible if we approached each moment with optimistic glee. Nonetheless, it is always we ourselves who either allow for or close off the possibilities of undergoing important changes.

External factors often play an important role in affecting our openness to change. Sometimes we meet very dynamic people who inspire us and we get caught up in their enthusiasm. These individuals make change sound very exciting. Other predictable people we encounter are boring and certainly do not stimulate any desire to change. Although it is ultimately we ourselves who establish the degree of openness at any moment, we still can, and indeed should, be affected by the behavior of others.

The difficulty of balancing change and non-change is compounded by the presence of anxiety. We all experience some degree of anxiety whenever faced with the possibility of making significant changes in our lives. To allow change is to give up the familiar and venture into strange and therefore potentially dangerous new experiences. However, this is the way we lift anchor. We all know who and where we are at any particular moment. We have a important sense of security in maintaining the familiar status quo, for we are anchored. To allow change is to open up ourselves to new risks. Even when people are living in horrific situations, such as regular abuse, they often are afraid to leave the familiar and venture forth into the unknown even if it is non-abusive. People who behave in such a manner and avoid change are living out the adage *I prefer the devil I know to the devil I do not know.*

At times we can briefly lose our bearings and even a sense of self whenever we embrace change and lift anchor. I vividly remember my first airplane trip, traveling from New York to Chicago in order to enter college. Midway between the two cities I had a moment of major panic as I asked myself *What in the blazes are you doing here and don't you realize what a mistake you may be making?* Thankfully, my choice turned out to be a good one.

Undergoing change threatens us because it undermines a sense of basic security. Whenever we start to make big important changes, we step into a scary void. What we are doing at that moment is abandoning our familiar self and opening up ourselves to becoming a different and as yet unknown person. Some existentialists describe anxiety as this powerful feeling of risk. Anxiety is the experienced threat of non-being. In the most general sense, non-being means that when you risk a change, you abandon and thereby destroy the "me" of the past moment. The most awful ultimate threat of non-being is the concrete threat of both our physical and psychological death.

At the moments when we sense the possibility of making meaningful changes, we will experience anxiety. For example, we can look at the image of the trapeze artist. The aerialist leaps off one bar and for a moment simply hangs in space. To make such a leap it is necessary to trust that one will be able to reach the next bar. We can all make such a leap and move forward, despite anxiety, if we trust that we will be able to recreate ourselves in the new situation. However, if we lack that basic self-trust, we will refuse to change and will keep ourselves very rigid.

In some circus acts, an aerialist flies toward another performer whose job it is to catch him/her. When we are raised in a healthy and loving family, we have a parent(s) who functions as such a *catcher*. We learn very early that the powerful adult will be there for us and will keep us from experiencing a free fall. If a child is raised without such caring, she/he will find it extremely difficult to make such a leap or to trust another person.

Continuing with the circus analogy, the effective psychotherapist can also be the *catcher* for the aerialist. Psychotherapy patients can come to trust that their therapists will be there for them to hold onto as they leap into the unknown of making new and important changes in their lives. Until they do see the therapist as a powerful and benevolent figure, psychotherapy will not be effective and healthy changes will not take place.

We all know anxiety is very uncomfortable, and sometimes we attempt to reduce the discomfort by refusing to make any decisions or take any action. The refusal to make life changes can often bring about a sense of temporary relief. However, not making decisions and refusing to take action may only perpetuate those problems which call for a resolution. In fact, delaying tactics are often particularly problematic, for it later becomes more difficult to make a decision if we have avoided decision-making at an earlier time. The inescapable truth is that a refusal to choose is still a choice. We are just as responsible for delaying action as we are for making wrong choices. We can always blame ourselves for making a wrong choice, and we can blame ourselves for refusing to make a choice. It is very difficult to avoid self-blame.

Existential psychologists say we create bigger and greater pain by refusing to let ourselves undergo changes. When we fail to allow for change, we transform existential anxiety (the natural threat of change) into neurotic anxiety (the irrational terror of what may befall us). Such internal machinations reduce our inherent power to confront the difficult human condition. To avoid anxiety, we generate even higher degrees of anxiety. We do not want to feel the threat of non-being which hovers about us whenever we consider making important changes. By not allowing ourselves to experience this dread, we create another unmanageable form of dread which takes the form of anxiety attacks, night terrors and phobias.

We cannot escape the pain and anxiety in the human condition. However, there is also a more powerful and important truth to embrace. When you find the courage to face your anxieties instead of succumbing to dread, you will own your greatest sense of personal triumph. When we ask ourselves what are we most proud of in our lives, it is likely we will remember particular moments when we took major risks despite feeling very anxious. By confronting and winning these difficult struggles, we transform ourselves into more powerful and better people. If we did not experience anxiety, there would never be such a sense of triumph. It is the triumph over ourselves which is most important to all of us. Experiencing such a triumph allows us to say we have led a valid and important life. When we take a leap into the void and take the risk of change, we are admirable and courageous. When we refuse to succumb to our anxiety and instead vow to take charge and move our lives forward, we validate the healthy and life-affirming sides of our personalities.

With each significant change that we make, we lose and abandon the person we had been. Even though we may transform ourselves into better people, some aspects of the "old me" are both familiar and comfortable and we, at times, would like to return to being that person. Indeed, there are times we will lose sight of the person we have become, and we will see and react to our world as if we were the old *me* rather than the stronger and newer *me*. Such reactions will feel familiar and comfortable, but they usually represent a diminution of the more powerful adult we have become.

To find the courage to make an important choice in the face of dread does not prevent any future problems. When we choose to open up ourselves to another by sharing our vulnerability, we carefully evaluate how we are being regarded. If we feel that we are being cared for, we usually will risk even more openness. When we begin to feel that the other does not care for us, we draw away.

Some of the choices we make will be good and validating, but other choices will prove wrong and painful. The best we can hope to do is evaluate the consequences of our choices and determine which were right and which were wrong. The evaluation process will lead us to take more risks or to back away from the initial choices. Even when we need to retreat, we can use that as a learning experience in new situations with other people. Hopefully, the pain of having made a poor choice will not prevent us from making other significant choices.

When we consider what we were like five, ten or 20 years ago, most of us realize we are now very different from that earlier person. For the most part we are happy with the changes. Nonetheless, there were heavy prices paid for these positive changes; we had to experience anxiety, we had to find the courage to endorse change, and we drew upon the healthy side of our personalities to do so. We are, therefore, inescapably both cursed and blessed with anxiety.

Coping With Our Human Limitations

Existential philosophers, novelists and psychologists all provide us with the realization that anxiety is a central, inevitable and necessary part of living. However, American culture has not embraced existential thinking. Even though there was a brief period of existential popularity in the 60s and 70s, the wonderful classic novels of Tolstoy, Dostoevsky, Sartre and Camus are rarely read today. These authors all provide insight into the human condition in ways that stimulate, provoke and enrich us. I was privileged to teach a course entitled the Existential Movement with a dear friend and colleague, Ervin Brody. Ervin guided students through the existential literature while I tried to explain existential philosophy and psychology. The students and I both learned a great deal from Ervin as he elucidated major themes in existential literature which are echoed and developed in the writings of philosophers and psychologists.

A basic theme permeating much of existential literature, philosophy and psychology is that most humans spend their lives unaware of the importance of creating a meaningful, enriching and fulfilling existence. Instead, they remain preoccupied with the mundane aspects of living, engaged in a form of automaton conformity, rarely questioning the values and standards of their upbringing. By not challenging themselves, they fail to maximize their individuality, for they are afraid to develop their own special personal identity. Many people proceed through much of life in such a fashion. Ervin Brody described them as being asleep.

In many novels which focus on this existential theme, some major event usually occurs that lifts the person to new and different possibilities for living. Often it may be a brush with death or a form of major trauma which heightens their level of consciousness. In colloquial English we can speak of experiencing a wake-up call. These novels describe such wake-up calls, with the major question being how the protagonists behave after they have been so rudely awakened.

The admirable heroes are able to awaken from nonthinking, conformist behavior and become much more alive and authentic. They find the courage to move forward, regularly questioning whether to comply with particular societal standards. The heroes make significant life changes despite their anxiety. In so doing, they recreate themselves. We readers can and will admire such heroes who find the courage *to be*. In fact, many of us are inspired to emulate such courage which, I believe, was the novelist's intention.

These heroes are particularly admirable because they must actively counteract the strong pull *to go back to sleep*. Again, the fictional heroes lead us to question our own experiences. At times we, too, wish to forget we have the power to change ourselves. It is easier and less stressful to refuse a forward move and instead continue to live in a non-challenging, conformist manner.

Certainly it is not possible to be continually recreating ourselves and moving forward all the time. We must, at times, simply engage in repetitive and non-creative tasks. We all get stuck in traffic jams, we need to clean up our living space and take out the garbage. In other words, there are routine and necessary tasks that take up significant time in our lives. We also need to have what is colloquially called *down time* so our brains and bodies can relax without important challenges.

We must seek a balance between moving forward and recreating our selves while still engaging in everyday life and relaxation. The most gratifying human lives interconnect these different ways of living. Knowing when to embrace change and when to maintain the status quo requires insight, artfulness and, sometimes, simply luck.

The struggle between these different forces, standing still and moving forward, has been described in helpful and interesting ways by several existential philosophers and psychologists. Three different accounts of the basic human struggle are central in the writings of Karl Jaspers (1955), Viktor Frankl (1960) and Rollo May (1979). Karl Jaspers was a German psychiatrist whose fundamental interest in the human condition led him to turn away from the study of psychopathology toward a lengthy career as a philosopher. Jaspers recognized that much of the time humans will live in a routine and repetitive manner, responding to external pressures and demands in predictable ways, just as Pavlov's dogs became conditioned through experimental training. Jaspers called this type of living on automatic pilot as "functioning as empirical existence." He believed the discipline of psychology could effectively understand people who functioned in that manner. The strategies of behavioral psychology are often adequate for studying and treating humans who function at the level of empirical existence.

However, Jaspers also believed we could raise ourselves to attain a higher level of functioning which he called *existenz*. Reaching *existenz* requires a strong act of will as it necessitates finding the courage to recreate ourselves. To function as *existenz* is to no longer be a predictable being; you stop engaging in routine and predictable behavior. Living as *existenz* means our actions express the deepest levels of our innermost being, i.e., who we most essentially are. We are all aware of the many times we assume a social mask where we dress the right way, say the right things and speak to the right people. When we function as *existenz*, we do the opposite and drop all pretensions of social niceties. Living as *existenz* means we will recognize ourselves to be the only and sole chooser of whatever we will do. In the language of an earlier section, when we live as *existenz*, we are being verbs. In fact, Jaspers believed that when we function as *existenz*, we ultimately will recognize our being is composed of all the choices that we have made.

It is extraordinarily difficult, if not impossible, to continually function at the level of *existenz* for in *existenz* one has to suspend engaging in everyday and routine behaviors. To acknowledge that we are truly free to choose *all* of our actions is not only exhilarating but also very threatening. In this scenario we must recognize we are always the judge and jury of our actions. Continual struggle to be truly authentic awakens a strong need for some external validation. Accordingly, people who are at the level of *existenz* seek soul mates who are willing to accept them at their deepest levels. These truest friends regularly encourage and challenge us to continue facing difficult choices and further our self-development. Once individuals have functioned as *existenz,* they do not wish to fall back to living as empirical existence. Unfortunately, we have too many routine life demands and external pressures requiring our attention, which makes ongoing and sustained living as *existenz* impossible. The best strategy one can hope for is to frequently move between functioning as empirical existence and as *existenz.*

Jaspers theorized a level for humans functioning beyond the level of *existenz.* He believed one can experience moments transcending *existenz,* seeing beyond oneself into the existence of deity. However, we can only have momentary glimpses beyond ourselves into this sense of deity because we are only human and, therefore, incapable of fully knowing God.

Jaspers' theory helps us realize we can all strive to live at the level of *existenz*. A very simple, mundane example better explains what occurs as we move from living the repetitive predictable routine as empirical existence into living as *existenz*. When you are functioning as empirical existence, you will routinely answer the telephone every time it rings. The compulsion to answer the phone can be so strong that you may subscribe to a caller identification service so you can redial calls at your own leisure. With such a service, the person who automatically answered each phone ring may now decide to answer or not. By making this decision, the individual stops reacting as a conditioned organism and becomes free of that behavior. The person experiences the freedom to choose to act in a way different from previous actions. Not answering a telephone call, in and of itself, is not proof that a person is functioning at a high level of being, for many people regularly do not answer telephone calls. This example is relevant because central to our functioning at the level of *existenz* is the willingness to change ourselves. Whenever we realize that we can step out of the confines of the past, we are moving toward functioning as *existenz*. In so doing we are also more open to *becoming plumb*.

A second psychiatrist, Viktor Frankl (1963), was personally able to demonstrate the power of the human spirit by surviving the horrors of the concentration camp experience. In studying his fellow inmates, Frankl recognized that only those with a fierce will to live were able to withstand the terrible ordeal. These people were able to find meaning in their day-to-day experiences despite the severe restrictions imposed on their behavior. Frankl himself wanted to live to see his book published so that his therapeutic system called "logotherapy" could become known to the world.

The basic premise of Frankl's logotherapy is that all humans are in pursuit of finding meaning to their lives. He believed the logotherapist could help direct a patient toward finding the path to personal meaning. The three basic ways one can find meaning are 1) doing a deed; 2) experiencing a value; or 3) suffering.

When we are in a situation where we have full freedom to act, performing a deed is the simplest way of ultimately discovering meaning. We may not know beforehand which actions will prove fulfilling. By making choices, and sometimes through trial and error, we ultimately will discover what is personally very meaningful. We can also find meaning through contemplation. We can ponder the major issues of life, or we can empathically connect with another. We can find value in appreciating much of what is outside ourselves by discovering the greatness in the insight or accomplishments of others. In other words, when we experience great art, literature or music, we can know in the moment that we have experienced something very important and meaningful.

Even in times of tragedy it is possible to find meaning in pain. Frankl felt that when we suffer the death of a loved one, it is possible to recognize our pain affirms the value and importance of the deceased person. In one of his consultations he spoke with an aged man who was quite depressed over the demise of his life-long partner.

Frankl pointed out that by outliving his spouse, the patient spared his wife the pain of having to live the rest of her life alone. The patient immediately found this interpretation quite helpful and comforting. Of course, we would all prefer to find meaning by being able to take positive action rather than through loss, but we do not always have that opportunity available.

Frankl offers the possibility of finding value and meaning in any situation. He remained optimistic about life despite the fact that his family was murdered in the holocaust while he personally faced and dealt with the horrors of being a concentration camp inmate. Knowing his life experiences and those of so many other people needlessly victimized serves to remind me that I have been spared personal sorrow. Frankl shows us that we have the power to transform our despair into an affirmation of ourselves, a wonderful legacy he has left for us all.

We can be inspired by Frankl. Even when at a loss as to how to handle our lives and as we struggle over the choices, Frankl's words are consoling. We all need to search for meaning, and we need not despair if we do not know what that meaning is at any given moment. Life is about a search for meaning, not about being able to regularly feel that meaning at any particular moment. Accordingly, one can feel positive about the human struggle.

A third basic description of the human struggle was developed in the writings of Rollo May (1979). May was a psychologist and analyst who had several books on the best seller list. May believed that in the human condition we all face a basic inescapable dilemma—all people are simultaneously subjects and objects. Sometimes we are capable of taking action, making choices and moving forward (being subjects). At the same time we are regularly being acted upon by external forces we cannot essentially control (being objects). Forces of nature will affect us, and other people can victimize us or certainly interfere with our lives. We can be hired or fired, taxed, assaulted or ignored and, at best, we may only be able to adjust or accommodate to these different actions. We cannot prevent these forces from operating upon us.

Because we are both subjects and objects, we can only have limited control over our lives. Rollo May understood that life can feel less stressful if one simply abandons the recognition of being a subject and proceeds through life as a powerless object. However, if we make such a choice, we are violating our basic nature. On the other hand, it would be a very destructive illusion to view ourselves as always being a subject who should be able to control both internal and external forces. At times we all experience the difficulty of recognizing what is possible for us to do and thereby we may feel essentially powerless. In those instances we mistakenly believe we are nouns and lose sight of the truth that we still are at that time irrefutably verbs. The struggle of being simultaneously subject and object is best expressed by the serenity prayer regularly recited at the meetings of Alcoholics Anonymous—"God, grant me the serenity to accept the things I cannot change, the courage to change the things I can, and the wisdom to know the difference."

May (1979) said when we recognize the dilemma of being simultaneously powerful and powerless, we can "pause between stimulus and response and see that we are the determined one." First we understand that we have been shaped both by external events and by other people. At that point we implicitly begin to acknowledge that we no longer have to function as conditioned beings. When we see we have been automatically giving the same learned responses to similar situations, we can then also immediately know there are other possible ways to respond. This allows us to see ourselves differently and recognize we have some power to change our response patterns.

The knowledge of when we have much power and when we have very limited power is very important as we steer our own way through the world. We have to come to terms with the many instances in which we are powerless. At the same time we need to admit that on occasion we may have had more power than we previously thought. In my lifetime I have seen seemingly all-powerful and cruel dictatorships toppled and oppressive regimes deposed. I and others had erroneously believed the population in these countries would never be free of tyranny. My point is that good reasons for optimism exist even when we have difficulty seeing the positive signs.

Nonetheless, awful things will ultimately happen to all of us and to those we hold dear. The best we can do in the meantime is to cherish our power in the immediacy of the now. We can follow the ideas of Jaspers and reach toward functioning as *existenz*. We can utilize the insights of Rollo May and attempt to balance functioning as a subject and an object, which will strengthen the subject side of ourselves. When we do face tragedy, we must still attempt to find meaning in our reactions to these terrible events, as Frankl suggests. In the very acts of striving to maximize living as subjects, reaching for *existenz* and seeking meaning, we can find true comfort in this very real and authentic human struggle.

9/11

Rollo May (1979) stated that at times in our lives we will all be powerless objects. His realization was dramatically and tragically demonstrated in the events of September 11, 2001. Thousands of innocent people perished through the destructive actions of fanatics. Most of those victims were afforded no viable option as they were trapped on the highest floors of the World Trade Center with no possible escape. Others working on lower floors could and did escape because they ignored a particular bureaucratic message urging them to remain at their desks. The gallant efforts of the police and fire department saved hundreds but, unfortunately, many of these heroes perished when the Twin Towers collapsed. Passengers on one of the airplanes were also able to resist the hijackers. They caused their plane to crash onto uninhabited ground rather than allow the terrorists to destroy more human lives by striking another major public building.

When these thousands in the World Trade Center were transformed into helpless objects, others immediately began to come to their aid, affirming our human capacity to function as subjects. Many others far away from Ground Zero also demonstrated that they, too, could be helpful. Enormous amounts of blood and money were donated. Volunteers gave time, food and clothes while still others provided free services for victims and their families. Our country experienced a surge of patriotism unseen since World War II. Millions of American flags were bought and flown at many households. The country strongly and completely united behind the president in this new war against terrorism.

The date 9/11 was implicitly transformed into 9-1-1, the national phone number we use for emergency assistance. Most Americans felt a strong need to contribute and to make a positive difference. It was intolerable to accept that we were only objects who could easily be destroyed. As a nation we resolved that we would do all in our power to ensure that such destruction would not happen again. We are, after all, subjects as well as objects; and we have a need to affirm our power whenever possible. Under conditions of threat, our healthy side, which affirms the value of human life, demands that we not simply submit, but that we rise up again, rebuild and move forward after we have been attacked.

Nonetheless, even though people mustered the courage to fight back against evil, many of us also began to experience increased dread and depression. It is indeed natural and normal to feel both anxiety and depression when one has experienced such extreme threats. Because of the large scale destruction of human life, the

Americans' reaction to this nightmare echoed much of the world's reaction to the systematic annihilation of human beings perpetrated by the Nazis. Facing the horror of the mass killings by Nazis, Sartre (1956) echoed Nietzsche's statement that *God is dead*. Many other Europeans who saw their countries ravaged and their fellow citizens enslaved and murdered also lost faith and a sense of personal meaning during those calamities. The same feelings of anxiety and depression are regularly experienced in countries such as Cambodia, Rwanda, Sudan, Bosnia and much of southeast Asia when the population fears for its own survival.

The destruction of the World Trade Center forced most Americans to face the unthinkable, namely, that we could be helpless victims at the hands of terrorists. Living in the most affluent and supposedly the safest country in the world, we had not previously entertained such incredibly depressing thoughts. However, Americans who are members of minority groups have not had the same lifelong illusions of being safe. They well knew, either personally or through their family history, that the world has not been safe for them or for their ethnic or religious group. With the collapse of the Twin Towers, most Americans, especially those living in proximity to New York City, found their illusion of safety very much shattered.

As a result, anxiety took over many people's lives. They became afraid to leave home and would not travel on airplanes or visit cities. The 9/11 massacre also reactivated the earlier anxieties and traumas experienced in people's developmental histories. As such, there was an observable increase in the various coping techniques that individuals use to deal with their underlying anxieties. A significant increase in the consumption of alcoholic beverages in the months following that devastation was well documented. I would have to believe there was a comparable increase in the use of illegal drugs as well. Furthermore, there was a startling increase in the amount of guns and ammunition sold in the months following the attacks.

The events of 9/11 caused a national trauma which became compounded a few weeks later by the detection of mail contaminated by the deadly poison anthrax. Healing from such traumas takes a long period of time. These events point out the inescapable human dilemma of our being simultaneously subject and object; they also served to awaken the "sleeper" in the American populace. Most specifically, we had to definitively face the fact that we could not know everything or be in control of everything. No one other than ourselves could make our world safe. Therefore, we were overcome by periods of anxiety and developed different strategies to gain some sense of reassurance. Many people became incessant watchers of cable news to feel informed and, in some small measure, in control of what was happening. Yet the continual watching of television news kept people at home and isolated and, therefore, made it more difficult to heal fully.

This national tragedy also left us with the basic realization that our lives are finite and can end without even a moment's notice. This is, of course, the most depressing and demoralizing realization possible. But it is also a very basic truth about our human condition. Nonetheless, it is a realization we do not want to keep in the forefront of our minds. To continually be aware of our impending death would render us immobile and unable to effectively attend to the demands of everyday life.

The psychologist Abraham Maslow (1954) stated that the range of human needs is experienced in a hierarchy. We have a very basic need for safety. When we have difficulty in finding ways of being safe, we focus our existence upon seeking more safety. Under such conditions it is only the very rare individual who will be able to address other and what Maslow labeled as higher level needs. Specifically, when we are in pursuit of feeling safe, we no longer focus upon having love or self-esteem needs met. Comparably, we do not engage in higher level self-development (what Maslow called self-actualization) when our safety needs remain unsatisfied.

Suddenly and unexpectedly having to face our inescapable vulnerability makes most of us feel immediately disoriented. This reality is also likely to make us feel depressed. It is crucial to realize that people can work their way out of such depression, but it is always a major struggle for when we are depressed, we feel powerless. Those who are able to move forward in the wake of a calamity are responding to this threat out of the healthy side of the personality.

The unhealthy side of the personality may bring about an increase in drug and alcohol use after exposure to trauma. On the other hand, the healthy side of the personality may produce attempts to connect with others, to give and receive support, to increase one's level of volunteering and to heighten one's sense of patriotism. Each specific response to trauma can easily be catalogued as coming from either the healthy or the unhealthy side.

However, it is very difficult for the healthy side of our personality to sustain control in the days and weeks following any severe trauma. In particular, many of us know these feelings from either being in a car accident or narrowly escaping one. These "after accident feelings" are considered post traumatic stress reactions. When automobile drivers recognize the presence of imminent danger, they usually are able to take swift and effective action to prevent injury. However, after the drivers have successfully avoided the accident, they often are flooded with anxious feelings. Sometimes the anxiety lasts only a few hours or days, but for others the anxiety can persist unabated over time.

After major trauma, most people frequently re-experience both anxiety and depression for several months. During this time an ongoing battle is waged between the healthy and unhealthy sides of the personality. The unhealthy side wants us to languish in despair while the healthy side calls to move forward with life. When the healthy side of the personality is fundamentally strong, one is able to successfully move forward in time. When the unhealthy side of the personality is very strong, it takes much longer for a person to resolve the pain-induced trauma.

All trauma can make us see we have not been fully participating in life and not appreciating the good in our lives. Stated in the language of Jaspers, we realize we have been living on the level of emperical existence rather than as *existenz*. As people recognize that life can be taken away at a moment's notice, they also glimpse the possibility of moving to the higher level of more authentic functioning. You become conscious of the importance of each moment, the value of being connected to others, and how precious your life really is. This recognition can also be a positive awakening that promises a new beginning, which represents the work of the healthy side of the personality.

Many individuals received assistance for post traumatic stress disorder after the destruction of the World Trade Center. Certainly, much of the general population was traumatized whether they lived near or far away from Ground Zero. Many people blame themselves for surviving when others perished and must now deal with survivor guilt. The unhealthy side of the personality is well able to twist the facts of a trauma into a cause for self-blame. One can be the victim of internal attack for a lack of sufficient planning, for not having seized lost opportunities and for not having made one's life outstanding.

For each of us to come to terms with such traumatic events, we must accept the basic limitations of our human condition. As uncomfortable as it is to *know* we will always be vulnerable, we can resolve to remain psychologically awake. *Knowing* we have the power to choose to make our lives more meaningful reminds us that we can reach for functioning at the level of *existenz*. Implementing such a resolution requires courage and a significant amount of will power. But that is where we can find consolation and even peace.

Another way of describing positive resolution to trauma is found again in the writings of Viktor Frankl. We especially need to find meaning when we face senseless destruction of human life. We need to struggle either to reaffirm the meaning that our life has had or to dedicate ourselves to finding new and important meanings for our lives. As stated earlier, Frankl said we can find meaning through activity, through experiencing a value and through suffering.

To find such deep meaning requires the use of our will to affirm the value of life. It is difficult to have positive feelings after a trauma, but we need to find the courage to move our life forward. Many people were heartened by the caring responses of others after the tragedy of the World Trade Center. Feeling well-connected with others is not only reassuring but also provides us with much personal strength. The solace provided by another is not only of great assistance in facing trauma but also a vital component in effective psychotherapy. The caring of others is a major contributor to the healing process.

When we face loss, we feel very much alone. Being offered solace and connection is therapeutic and necessary. Helping each other through pain is one of our most precious qualities. Reconnecting and rebuilding are strong affirmations of our basic life force.

On Facing Death

The most difficult event we have to face in life is death. Whenever we ponder the possibility of death, we are filled with some combination of anxiety and depression. Thinking about death makes us feel alone and vulnerable with no escape from such pain. The anticipation of death fills us with dread and can immobilize us. Some people become so terrified about facing their ultimate death that the terror prevents them from living a full life. Early in my professional training I learned that many psychoanalysts dismissed the validity of peoples' fear of death by saying that such fears were defenses against other anxieties. Such a conception may have been the analyst's defense against having to deal with both the patient's fear of death as well as a personal death fear. Because we humans love life we become both afraid and angry about our ultimate death.

We cannot find a fully satisfying way to deal with the fact that death will happen. We all want to banish thoughts of death from our minds and from our reality. However, because death is always around us in some fashion, we cannot ignore it. If you avoid dealing with the inevitability of death, you will create additional serious problems for yourself.

It is built into our nature to hate death. We humans are life forces, and death will ultimately annihilate us. Therefore, at the core of our being, we rail against death, and our anger is an affirmation of our being. We can only know how important and valuable life truly is because we recognize that it will end. We draw upon dialectic reasoning, or the recognition of opposites, as our way of fully understanding any concept or experience. Comparably, death can be understood and best dealt with through the recognition and affirmation of life.

I wrote the first draft of this section about death on the day that our dear dog Fiona died. Many of us, after facing the death of a loved person or a loved pet, need in some way to commemorate what we have loved and then lost. I needed to write about Fiona on the day she died because that was one way I could keep a part of her alive.

Earlier in my life after my own parents died, I was compelled to write a short history of each of their lives as well. I needed to make a record of the kind of people they were so my children would have a fuller understanding of my parents. Such a record would enable my grandchildren to in some way know what kind and loving people my parents were. Both of my parents died years before my own grandchildren were born. The increased popularity of discovering family history and writing family trees is a widespread attempt to own one's own historical lineage. It is one way of keeping death from fully annihilating us.

In the face of death I feel, like most other people, an overpowering need to affirm life. Whenever we hear of someone's death, we have a need to discover why the death happened. We want to hear that people who died did not take good care of themselves or had a bad genetic make-up or at least were very old and, therefore, possibly ready to die. If we find an affirmative answer to any one of these questions, we can then feel somewhat reassured. We want to be deceived into believing there was a good reason for the death and that it does not simply happen to anyone.

Unfortunately, we really know that death does "just happen." Death is so horrible to face that we want to avoid it. When anyone we love dies, it seems so utterly unfair. We want life to go on forever. When we know that a loved one is about to die, most of us, believers or atheists, try to make deals with a god so that death can be avoided. However, the ugly truth is that we are human, and humans have a time-limited existence. Life is limited for all the people we love. Life is limited for the people we do not love as well. Unfortunately and tragically, life is also limited for ourselves.

When we are forced to deal with the reality of death, we find the people who are nearest and dearest to us typically reach out with love and compassion. People are able to share their innermost feelings with others when they know how much the person is hurting. By affirming our love and connections with others, our life force says *to hell with death* and we *know* death will never fully triumph.

Death robs us of those we love. At some level of our being we are angry because so many people and animals we have loved were taken away from us by death. To be sad when death happens is natural. To hate death is also natural and healthy because we humans are life-affirming creatures. I will always hate death because that hatred embodies my love of life. We cannot love fully without allowing ourselves to be able to hate fully what is hateful. Again, I see the necessity of dialectic reasoning and experience.

Yet I also recognize that there can come a time when many of us are ready to die. What we all hope for is a long life, free of disease and pain, where we simply do not wake up one morning in our old age. Too many are not so lucky and have to endure much suffering before life ends. Regardless of how death will happen, we need to be able to accept the inevitability of our death, not only at a rational level but at an emotional level as well. We can and need to fight to sustain our lives as long as possible, but we also can best win these battles when we know that we cannot hold on to life forever.

It is imperative that we draw upon our life force, the healthy side of our personality, to deal with the inevitability of death. That powerful life force demands we first acknowledge that we are alive now, at this point in time, and that feeling fully alive is truly wonderful. As we more fully participate in living in the now, we can better recognize that we have the power of choice. We have the ability to control and even redirect the course of our lives. We then will become more able to use the immediate moment to fully express and develop who and how we would like to become.

When we do face the inevitability of death, we feel an overpowering need to affirm ourselves, to better express our personal values and beliefs. We need to make our lives become the fullest expression of our being because in that manner, we most fully affirm life. We all will have to face the terrible pain of the loss of loved ones, and that grief and anguish will reach down to the core of our being. Nonetheless, death is most awful when the victim has never found the courage to fully face and to create a personally meaningful life.

Viktor Frankl (1963) said that only by facing and accepting the inevitability of death will we be able to make our lives meaningful. He added that if there were no time constraints upon human life, no decision could ever be crucial as it could always be reversed. If life went on forever, we could learn to play the piano in the next 100 years or get divorced 200 years in the future.

However as we all know, we have a limited life span which makes it imperative we use our time productively. We cannot live as if each day were our last day on earth because that would be too overwhelming and might very well lead to irresponsible behavior. On the other hand, we do need to lead our lives by recognizing from time to time that ultimately life will come to an end. This recognition enables us to make each day count. At the very least it will help us see the beauty and wonder present in the everyday world.

It is not difficult to find beauty or meaning in a part of the day if we allow ourselves to be open to the world. A day is important whenever we can appreciate any part of it. The day becomes meaningful to us because we have used our energies effectively or have made in some manner the particular day worthwhile. We all have the potential power to make our existence meaningful.

When we first face the inevitability of death, we are confronted with how powerless we truly are. However, once we truly accept the utter powerlessness of dying, we can accept the pain and more fully affirm our lives by making more willful choices. Once again, because we know deep dread and despair, we can also own the strength of reshaping the nature of our existence. As a result, we become extraordinarily powerful only after we have faced our ultimate powerlessness.

I know this is the basic truth of my own life. I have been living my life, making personally meaningful choices. My life has been spent affirming my values and my love of life. I have been able to help create and to foster life. I have been given the gift of love and have been able to give it back to others. My life has been so full of meaning for me that I will never be fully obliterated by death. I will ultimately lose my life, but the life I have led is an affirmation of my being which can never be destroyed.

You can recognize that you, too, can choose and create a life that is important, gratifying and personally meaningful. The sooner you own the capacity and ability to shape your life, the more options you have at your disposal. We conquer death by the affirmation of our own lives and by affirming the importance of the lives of loved ones who are no longer with us. Such affirmation is our true antidote to death. I keep the memories of all my loved ones alive, and I know that ultimately we will all be reunited once my own final anchor has been lifted.

Conformity, Group Participation and Individuality

Can you imagine what your life would have been like if all your elementary school classmates had been non-judgmental people who simply accepted you as well as accepted each other? We all would have felt much less tension if the majority attitude had been "do your own thing and we will applaud you for it." It is ironic that virtually all of us want to receive that kind of acceptance, but few are actually given such approval. Sullivan (1953) said it is not until children reach 10 to 12 years of age that they become capable of providing full and complete acceptance of another human being. Furthermore, he believed it was not until the late teenage years that people were capable of a truly intimate relationship with someone of the opposite sex. The writings of Sullivan serve to affirm our implicit recognition that it is very difficult to find both peers or potential lovers who will provide us with full acceptance.

We all encountered peer criticism and rejection in our early years of elementary school. We can probably recall the bullies we had to deal with and the occasions when it seemed that all of our classmates laughed and made fun of us. It was very upsetting to become an unwilling target, especially when we knew we had not done anything to provoke it. Finding oneself as the scapegoat during elementary school is an experience that few of us can forget. It is also an experience that few of us were ever able to avoid. Perhaps for that reason, many of us have enjoyed the Charlie Brown character in the Peanuts comic strip because we can remember the times when we, too, felt like losers.

During elementary school we have our first major experience of dealing with a crowd. Rarely will a group of school-age children attend to the needs of any one individual. They all too often look for an easy target to vent their personal frustrations. The pressure exerted by the group on any one individual can be enormous; and especially as children, we are likely to conform to that external pressure. Consequently, many children demand their parents buy them the *right clothes* that have the *right color* and the *right label.* Wearing the right clothes is absolutely essential in elementary school years; it functions as a protective technique in order to avoid ridicule.

Because of the power of peer pressure, children frequently adopt the crowd mentality and become judgmental of others while, correspondingly, endorsing the standards of the in-group. In elementary school we first learn the importance of conformity as an important survival mechanism.

Some of us learn the lesson too well and automatically continue to conform to whatever seems to be the majority position. Others ultimately learn to balance individual development while demonstrating some deference to the demands of the larger group.

Interpersonal success in elementary and high school is often easiest if you are in with a particular crowd and adopt the dress, attitudes and behaviors of that group. The elementary school years are the time of the most powerful forms of peer pressures; and again most of us can clearly remember instances where we believed expression of our own individual positions would produce ridicule. Creating a scapegoat and ostracizing others is most frequently done in elementary school. These behaviors, however, often persist into high school where cliques regularly stereotype and shun others. The old adage — the best defense is a strong offense— has, unfortunately, been adopted as a code of conduct by far too many people.

As adolescents we usually faced many pressures from peers: to drink, to smoke, to experiment with the current fashion drugs as well as be sexually active. Many may also have been ostracized for being too smart, too weird, too thin, too fat, too quiet, too loud or for being a geek. We can all probably remember occasions when we kept quiet although we would have preferred to speak up. However, one deferred to the crowd because it was easier not to assert an individual opinion.

On the other hand, there were times when each of us did defy the crowd and followed our own path. Good friends, or *chums* in the language of Sullivan (1953), usually help in this behavior because they often encourage us to express our point of view or at the very least, respect us when we voice a viewpoint different from their own. Good friends provide a level of acceptance and support which gives us the courage to further develop our individuality.

Unfortunately, our larger culture primarily devalues individual expression and favors conformity. Therefore, even though we hope to be loved for being ourselves, we are likely to feel some anxiety whenever we consider making a controversial comment. Many children are so frightened at the prospect of peer disapproval in elementary school that they do not develop a personal viewpoint and remain intimidated even as they pass into adulthood.

People who do remain intimidated by peer disapproval frequently ask *what will other people think* before taking any action. When you choose a course of behavior because of the potential reactions of others, you lock yourself into conformist behavior. This kind of thinking and action blocks individual development because your personal opinion is given little credence. As a result, this kind of person more frequently exhibits stereotypic behavior and systematically avoids action which could be considered controversial.

For some children, individual expression was stifled in their early upbringing before they attended any school. In these instances one or both parents did not permit the child to adopt ideas which were at variance with the parental position. When children are severely punished or psychologically abandoned for expressing their own needs or viewpoints, they quickly learn that it is too dangerous to do anything that might provoke a reprimand. As a result, they become inhibited and do not risk developing their own individuality.

Carl Rogers' (1951) theory on the causes of maladjustment espoused such a point of view. He believed that adjustment problems began when individuals chose how to think and how to behave in order to be liked by significant others. He attributed this behavior to what he called the *need for positive regard*. Rogers asserted it could become the most powerful need in the personality, even stronger than the *need for self-actualization*, the need to further one's personal development. Rogers believed that if the psychotherapist provided positive regard on an unconditional basis, the client would be able to choose behavior patterns to satisfy the need for self-actualization instead of continuing to function in ways designed to produce positive regard.

Even when the home environment supports healthy individual development, children soon learn that individual expression can lead to trouble. I personally believe that with a supportive home environment, children can often find the strength to further the expression of their individuality. However, peers become especially important during elementary school so that even the healthiest child must struggle to find a balance between being accepted and expressing his/her uniqueness. Finding an effective balance between these two behavior patterns is a problem many people struggle with through life. We all need to receive some degree of peer acceptance. The less accepted a person feels, the more vulnerable she/he is to external pressure.

According to Otto Rank (1968), the major life task is the struggle between expressing individuality and conforming to the wishes of the group. Rank believed that people sense if they are too much their own person, they will be abandoned by others and isolated. On the other hand, if they simply and generally try to satisfy the wishes of others, they will fear for the destruction of their individuality. Rank called these two fears the fear of life and the fear of death, first both experienced in our early years. He believed the only way to manage balancing these two fears was through the development of a strong personal will.

Rank reminds us that we all have a need to be well-connected with and affirmed by others. We humans are very much social creatures, and participation with others is an important expression of who and what we are. We form our first friendships because of shared interests; and, as we mature, we join different groups because we have beliefs or passions in common with the group. In high school we join particular clubs because they focus upon an interest that we personally endorse. We join teams because they play the sport we enjoy playing. When a sports team from our locale wins a big game, many of us feel as if we, too, are a part of that triumph. We may bask in our ethnic heritage and endorse particular forms of nationalism. We become Republicans or Democrats and then share certain philosophies with other Republicans and Democrats. Religious participation is another area in which we share with and connect to others.

Many sociologists consider these different affiliations as social roles and believe that one's sense of identity comes from the various roles that he/she plays. To be successful, it is necessary to both know and play specific social roles such as employee, student, etc. However, adopting particular role behaviors needs to be part of a wide repertoire of possible activities. The emotionally healthy individual engages in certain common behavior patterns as simply one particular expression of a unique personal identity. For example, one can be a Republican and primarily agree with the views of a Republican president but still voice disagreement with particular positions that a president has taken. Automatic agreement with whatever a president promotes is simply conforming to the social or political group. Such a person has abandoned expressing individuality.

Herein lies the particular difficulty that we all face. We need and like to have certain types of memberships in different groups. We are likely to endorse a number of the positions taken by these groups, which is why we joined. However, because we each have our own individual viewpoints, we are likely to disagree with some of the group's beliefs. When we are able to retain our beliefs in opposition to the group, we also maintain our individuality. When we submerge our beliefs to those of the group, we become conformists and diminish our own sense of self. We need to belong, but we must not abandon our individuality for the sake of group acceptance. On the other hand, we also must temper the strength of our need to superimpose our views upon the group or else we can destroy our relationships with the other members.

I personally agree with Rank that we all need to develop our *will* in order to balance between these two opposing tendencies. Through the *will* we then are able to become the self-actualized self. However, to fully develop the *will,* we need to receive strong affirmation from others, either in the current situation or in our earlier years. Many people have received that deep affirmation from parental figures or from other powerful figures encountered as children. Some first received such affirmation from close friends or lovers, while still others have never received this kind of positive regard.

In the typical course of human development, when the healthy side of the child is not primarily affirmed by the parents, the child unfortunately begins to believe that no one will ever provide such love or affirmation. As a result, these children start to behave in ways that distance them from others, making it difficult or impossible for anyone to be able to reach out and provide such crucial affirmation. In such instances it becomes the task of the psychotherapist to provide that affirmation and thereby help further the development of individuality.

When entering college, you meet many new people and often discover that some do provide validation and acceptance. Self-expression becomes so much easier when we find another person who is interested in hearing what we have to say and is willing to probe and even challenge our thoughts in a healthy way. In college it was wonderful fun to stay up most of the night talking about the world, the afterlife, religion, sex, our parents, our upbringing and whatever else came to mind. These talks broadened our perspective and were one of the most important parts of the college experience for me.

Open discussions with thoughtful peers often help us to better clarify our own values. These talks also make us recognize how our views differ. Through the open exchange of ideas, we recognize that even as we differ from friends and family, we can still like and respect them. Through both late-night dormitory discussions as well as in some college classrooms, we more systematically probe the big and important questions about life. Those of us who developed such deep friendship patterns in college are usually able as adults to find similar friends who provide both challenge and acceptance for us. Isolation in college is likely to eliminate seeking out such friendship patterns in later life.

Attending college typically frees one from virtually all parental controls. The student demonstrations and rebellions of the 60s prompted colleges to abandon the concept of functioning *in loco parentis,* or as parental substitutes. For many students, college then primarily became a time to rebel by immersing themselves in ongoing pleasures. College students certainly need to engage in some form of rebellion as they move into full adult status. On the other hand, college offers more than the mere opportunity to rebel, for it is also the best time and place for the healthy side of the personality to develop. If the unhealthy side of the personality is dominant, the college experience can become a large experiment in self-destruction.

Some students use the college experience as a prime opportunity for systematically challenging authority. Indeed, if authority is not challenged in late adolescence, it is highly unlikely that one will ever take a position against the crowd or be able to disagree with the boss. If you are unable to disagree with or to challenge authority, you remain the conformist child. However, regular and indiscriminate challenging of authority is also childish, albeit the behavior of a defiant child. Neither pattern is healthy. Finding a balance between the two is, I believe, an important task of the late adolescent and early adult years.

The struggle among individuality, group participation and conformity is very much heightened during the college years. On the one hand, the student is now living with peers rather than parents, and that makes peer acceptance more powerful. On the other hand, students are exposed to new ideas and impressive people who may assume positions very different from peers. The college student then has to decide among peers, teachers and authors, or one's own prior view, as to what holds the greatest weight or validity. Furthermore, the college student needs to pose this question about many different content issues. In other words, the task is to evaluate each position independently. As students focus upon thinking for themselves, they realize that certain authorities are sometimes correct and sometimes wrong on certain topics. No one can be totally wrong about everything, nor can they be totally right on everything. Theoretically, life would be easier with an indisputable expert we could consult for all the answers, but such an expert does not exist. If we found someone who assumed such a role and we believed this person was indeed correct, we would again be placing ourselves in a childlike position. It might feel comfortable in the moment, but such dependency is not healthy.

The most we can hope for is to discover what is right for each of us at any one particular moment. We need to implicitly accept, or place in the back of our mind, that our beliefs and positions can and will change over time. The person we meet in college who seems to be absolutely perfect for us and whom we love fully and passionately, will probably either discard us or we will discard him/her. Rarely do we successfully keep our first loves. One truth we can be sure of is that we cannot be fully sure of everything.

The implicit recognition that we cannot have true certainty does pull us toward conformity. Functioning as a member of a crowd is so much more immediately comfortable. When we feel the strong pull of the group, we can simply accept what the group decides and not have to arrive at an independent position. Certainly there are times when we all feel sorely tempted to turn off our minds. In fact, there are times when the healthiest thing to do is not to think but instead simply to play and escape from ongoing deep contemplation. Not thinking in the moment is sometimes necessary, but conformity for the sake of conformity is a poor alternative.

The basic problem with being a conformist is that any acceptance we receive from thinking, acting and dressing like the group is hollow; we gain a surface rather than a depth acceptance. As a result, when we behave like everyone else, we know that we are not *really* being accepted. Then we fear that if we risked expression of our *real* feelings, we might be rejected. Conformist behavior fails to make us feel truly *liked* because we all want to be liked and accepted for *being ourselves*. The conformist behaves in order to be liked, and this is a negation of individual expression.

As we each try to balance individuality, social participation and conformity, we will be trying to maintain proper steering, similar to computer games where the spaceship travels through moving obstacles. Alertness to obstacles and the ability to change paths is the essential key to winning the computer game. The same flexible attitude is necessary for managing a satisfying life style. We each have to steer our own vehicle, but we also have to use automatic pilot to deeply relax and enjoy the experience of simply being alive.

In fact, a potential danger exists. If you transform the basic need to control your life into a constant demand to find the best or most productive way to spend each day, you will be very uncomfortable. In other words, an obsessive need to live one's life the *right* way can be as destructive as the refusal to chart one's own course. You need to assume the role of primary decision-maker in your own life while also accepting the truth that some of these decisions may prove to be wrong. You will make significant errors in some of your choices, and you must accept these errors without resorting to massive self-punishment. If we are reasonable with ourselves, we will be able to effectively refine and reformulate our positions.

Finding one's way is never a straight line but rather a path of stops, starts and wrong turns. The journey can be delightful and fun as long as narcissism does not insist you know the right path beforehand. Again, when a significant person supports our individuality and tolerates our mistakes, we can maintain self-confidence. When you feel alone, it is very difficult to continue to trust your individuality. Nonetheless, at those times we still need to believe and hope that a supportive person will enter our lives. In fact, the more we are willing to develop and express our own individuality, the more likely it is that we will meet someone who will truly love and respect us.

Existentialists recognize that conformity stifles one's individuality, and some of these authors consider conformity to be a form of non-being or death. The attack upon conformist behavior too often fails to recognize the profound social needs paramount in us all. At times conformity is necessary and helpful because it suits particular needs and choices. In such instances where you and the group agree on proposed action, your behavior need not be labeled as conformist. However, automatic conformity is as destructive as automatic rebellion. By accepting the validity of dialectic thinking, we realize that individuality cannot and need not be continually expressed. Sometimes it is wise to follow the demands of the crowd because some issues are not worth fighting over. Therefore, what we all need to do is to find a comfortable and healthy balance between conforming and expressing individuality. These ongoing decisions will continue to be made throughout the course of our lives. Keeping ourselves aware that we are regularly making choices to satisfy both our social and our individualized needs gives us the insight to select both wisely and well.

On Morality

People typically lead their lives by following some basic principles such as *A bird in the hand is worth two in the bush,* or *It is better to have loved and lost than to have never loved at all.* Some formulas for living can be quite deliberate such as *I want to get the most money that I can* or *I want to have as many sex partners as possible.* However, most of the time we do not consciously review or examine our principles. Rather, we simply behave in ways that affirm our fundamental schemes for living. In other words, we all have and follow an implicit philosophy of life although most people would find it very difficult to articulate their actual philosophy.

As expected, philosophers first set out to describe and understand the different approaches or philosophies of life that we humans can follow. A very brief discussion of a few of these ideas is helpful in providing a backdrop for discovering one's own approach to living. Kierkegaard (Jolivet, 1951) thought that in the early phases of our lives, all of us pursue and will do whatever we sense will please us. Some 80 years later Freud labeled such behavior as following the pleasure principle. According to Kierkegaard, people who continue the pursuit of pleasure are living at what he called the aesthetic stage. The basic principle behind the actions of aesthetes is to continue to find bigger and better pleasures. Aesthetes typically live just for the moment and have much difficulty in both tolerating frustration and long-term planning. For Kierkegaard, the only way to stop living as an aesthete and move to a higher level of functioning was through a strong exercise of personal will. With sufficient desire or enough will power, one's basic approach to life could be changed.

When people transform themselves and leave the aesthetic stage, they ascend to what Kierkegaard called the ethical stage. In the ethical stage people live out their lives by following their prescribed duty. Duty is usually defined by the teachings of one's religion, though it could probably also be defined by following the principles and rules of the prevailing society. To live at the ethical stage is to do what is *right* and to avoid doing what is *wrong*. The task is to decide which rule for living best applies in each particular situation. Kierkegaard believed that people living at the ethical stage expect to be able to avoid pain and suffering because they are regularly doing the *right* things. They also expect to be well rewarded in the afterlife. When one experiences anguish and pain, despite consistently behaving ethically, the person will feel quite lost. In an attempt to resolve such pain, Kierkegard believes the person can feel the impetus to reach for an even higher level of functioning.

The third and highest level Kierkegaard described as functioning at the religious stage. This conception of religious is quite different from the ordinary definition. For Kierkegaard the truly religious person must decide what is right in any given situation and must also be willing to make some decisions at variance with the dictates of the formal religion. People who live at Kierkegaards's religious stage take enormous risks by following their own conscience. They are willing to make decisions which may defy standard religious doctrine. As they wrestle to find the truth, they are willing to ultimately justify their choices before their god. It is extraordinarily difficult to continue to function at this religious stage, because of the dread associated with realizing no one else can affirm that one's personal choices are, indeed, correct. Nonetheless, such people must continue to think and act for themselves despite the anguish which it may cause.

Today, almost 200 years after Kierkegaard, many people do not defer to religious teachings with the same unquestioning level of belief they did in his time. When individuals do not defer to the authority of higher institutions, they are then forced to think and decide for themselves what is right. Independent decision-making still can produce the same kind of anguish Kierkegaard described, as one cannot receive credible outside affirmation for an independent decision. By choosing to follow what most people advocate as being *correct*, the person can function at the ethical stage and use conformity to at least temporarily avoid feeling dread. However, according to Kierkegaards's paradigm, one cannot rise to the highest level of functioning if one does not think for oneself.

Anguish over making important decisions can be so abhorrent that an entire country or society may submit to the power of an authority figure as a way to avoid making difficult personal choices. Eric Fromm (1941) believed this path was taken by Germany in the 1930s. Fascism made individuals feel safe from independent decision-making, and most Germans chose conformity over individuality in supporting the Nazi regime. Existential writers after Kierkegaard essentially agree that we all face major dilemmas and potential dread whenever we attempt to decide on the right life path for us to follow. Although these writers use somewhat different terminology, they uphold the basic existential position; there is no valid universal scheme of what is right and what is wrong. Instead, they argue that we must each decide on what we personally believe is right and what is wrong. We need to be willing to change our beliefs as our experiences change, and we also need to respect others' rights to decide on what is right or wrong for each of them.

It is anxiety-provoking to decide independently how to be. Many people avoid such a struggle and simply conform to and adopt the position of the majority in order to feel some level of security. Most existential writers think such conforming behavior is a major impediment to the development of a personally meaningful sense of one's self. They advocate that we each find the courage to create a personal philosophy for living based upon what we believe to be valid principles. In so doing, we will be reaching for our highest level of being and expression.

Existential philosophers, novelists and psychotherapists consider it crucial to develop one's own creed or personal morality. Once you possess such a set of standards, it can guide and direct you toward a more meaningful and productive life. These standards or principles will function as ideals, personally endorsed as being vitally important for we have decided they are the *right* ways to behave. Whenever we fail to live according to these standards, we then know that our behavior was *wrong;* and we feel guilty for violating our personal standards.

Moral standards seem to have fallen out of vogue in this early part of the 21st century. Many Westerners function at the aesthetic stage or live according to the pleasure principle. Perhaps even more unsettling and troublesome is that self-indulgence is now frequently described as a morally justifiable code for living. A prevalent view today entitles individuals to do whatever they feel like doing; and, correspondingly, other people do not have the "right" to criticize anyone else's behavior. The dictum is to remain quiet and not hold others accountable for their offensive behavior. For example, when a person engages in behavior patterns injurious to others, these actions can always be rationalized. This reasoning essentially turns morality on its head because upholding and affirming a set of moral principles has become immoral itself. In other words, the worst or most immoral action now is to be overtly judgmental of another person's behavior.

Many noncritical individuals view themselves as quite humanitarian and interpersonally accepting members of our society. However, a refusal to be judgmental or critical is also an unwillingness to label particular behaviors wrong. Once we eliminate labeling certain actions *wrong,* we lose any rationale for labeling any behaviors *right.* This refusal to make judgments produces an implicit endorsement of any and all kinds of behaviors. For example, when we explain away heinous behaviors, such as rape or murder, because the perpetrator was also a victim of violence, we then eliminate necessary human accountability. It is imperative that atrocious behavior is labeled as atrocious, and individuals who engage in such actions should receive major sanctions for their actions. Because we live in a society of people, we must have rules for conducting behavior as well as consequences for violating these rules. For societies to survive, they must endorse one way of behavior as better over another. We may each personally disagree with some of these standards. However, most of us certainly realize that when we violate these standards, we are quite likely to face painful consequences. If we are comfortable disagreeing with these larger societal standards, we must be able to substitute our personal principles for consensual views and be willing to justify our position.

Living according to the pleasure principle or living at the aesthetic stage can involve a wide range of behaviors. One of the most popular manifestations is to focus upon the satisfaction of one's material wishes. Many Americans strive to make the most money, build the largest houses and indulge in the largest extravagances. Success is of crucial importance and is typically measured in material terms.

The overpowering need to be successful is quite evident even in elementary school and may continue throughout life. The desire to be successful can be quite healthy unless one chooses to be successful at any cost. A recent newspaper article reporting a survey measuring student honesty discovered that 70% of high school students admitted to cheating on their examinations in the past year, and 80% of the high achievers also admitted to cheating on tests. Cheating on examinations has apparently become normative behavior, and honesty is rare. The majority of students seem to believe that being successful is most important, and it does not matter what one does in order to receive those high grades.

Most of us implicitly sense that when an individual is dishonest in one way, it is quite likely that he/she will be dishonest in other ways. It would be foolish to trust such a person. A significant relationship with such a person is risky. We can anticipate that a person who cheats at school may cheat at marriage, on the job, and is quite likely to look for the easy way out of uncomfortable situations. If honesty and integrity are irrelevant concepts during one's youth, only some major self-accounting will cause the person to make profound changes in outlook. Otherwise, that personal code of morality which has endorsed self-indulgence will continue to be followed throughout life without hesitation.

Parents are the first to teach a code of conduct to their children. In other words, parents typically set the moral groundwork. In effective parenting, children are rewarded for following these rules by engaging in what is considered desirable behavior. Children are also punished for failing to follow these rules. Ideally, the child specifically learns which actions are *right* and which actions are *wrong* and internalizes that way of thinking. Parental rules are the first moral standards, supported for many children at their places of worship.

During adolescence individuals typically challenge the legitimacy of parental rules. These challenges are healthy and necessary, and they help teenagers move toward becoming their own person with a personal set of beliefs. When adolescents decide that childhood rules are in actuality wrong, they will rebel against and overthrow these rules. Teenage rebellion typically occurs first with the defiance of all rules. Stating that *no* rules are valid is often a first, but hopefully short, step towards full independence.

After adolescents overthrow the initial rules, however, they need to substitute new rules for the old ones. Although freedom from any rules is at first a wonderful and liberating feeling, one can also feel very lost with total freedom. If you continue to live without rules, it means you are functioning without any principles and therefore becoming amoral. When an adolescent begins to ask how he/she should be and how she/he should not be, the individual ultimately is likely to retain some of the principles or moral ideals from childhood. Teenagers often choose familiar standards for their behavior because these particular principles actually make good personal sense. They soon realize that some of the principles in their upbringing endure well under intense questioning.

Questioning and a willingness to change one's principles is an ongoing process that can profitably persist throughout our lives. It does not end with adolescence. As we mature and discover new life situations,.we often find some of our principles need to be changed for they no longer fit the person we have become. Not only is it important for us to be willing to question our current moral rules, but it is also necessary for us to be open to continue questioning and changing these standards. Failure to change our beliefs and our morality will cause us to become rigid. This struggle over what is right and what is wrong is not an easy process. As we struggle, sometimes we despair and other times feel an important sense of triumph. Once again we see the inescapable dialectic truths. To decide what is right, we must simultaneously decide what is wrong. One cannot exist without the other.

The development of one's own moral code has another major and positive consequence. If you decide what is *right* in the abstract, you are better able to know what is *right* for you in the immediate situation. We then can know what is the *right* thing to do, and we will feel a deep level of certainty about our correct course of action. In those moments of choice we are *being plumb*. It would be rare for a person to *be plumb* if that individual lacked a basic sense of what was personally right and wrong. Accordingly, a consistent personal moral code is regarded as the basic prerequisite for *becoming plumb*.

GUILT

Guilt, just like anxiety, is a very uncomfortable feeling. The feeling of guilt occurs whenever we do something we believe is wrong. Most of us wish we could avoid feeling guilty because we do not want to experience any kind of pain. Unfortunately, feeling guilty, just like feeling anxious, is a natural part of our human condition. There are only two possible ways for a person not to feel guilty. The first way would be always to think, feel and act in a manner consistent with your value system which, of course, is impossible to do. The other way to avoid feeling guilty would be to live without any set of personal expectations, goals or standards. People who have no goals cannot fail in their own eyes. Of course they cannot really succeed in any meaningful way either. They might do certain things very well, but if they are not invested in their performance, i.e., they have no expectations, then their success becomes irrelevant.

When we feel guilty, we are engaging in a form of self-blame. We blame ourselves for not acting the way that we *should have acted.* People who live without standards have no reason for self-blame which, therefore, keeps them free of guilt. No standards is far too high a price to pay to avoid feeling guilty, for to live one's life without a sense of what one ought to do or ought not to do would make for an aimless and empty existence.

Most of us first learned to feel guilty when we were small children. We were given specific rules to follow; and whenever we violated these rules, we were reprimanded by parental figures. Adults want their child to feel bad whenever the child breaks parental rules. In fact, the parents hope their children will feel so bad that they will no longer defy parental wishes. Parents instill guilt in the child so that these feelings of guilt will motivate the child to avoid behavior which the parents consider undesirable.

Children can and will break parental rules without feeling guilty. When the very young child is caught violating parental rules, the child is typically taught to say the two magic words, *I'm sorry,* which will makes things right again with the parent. The young child has not yet come to believe that specific behaviors are good and specific behaviors are bad in their own right. Instead, what the child can first learn and understand is that certain behaviors will be rewarded and other behaviors will lead to trouble. Only as children reach ages four to five are they able to accept these parental standards as valid. Healthy children then internalize these standards as basic definitions of what is right and what is wrong.

Children will begin to feel guilty when they violate these *correct* standards of behavior. In order to get rid of guilt feelings, the child may confess to the parent and thereby be granted forgiveness. In the earliest years of life, the child is in the position of answering to the parent; and it is the parent who can both instill guilt and grant forgiveness. It takes a number of years before children develop the concept of answering to themselves and becoming the primary monitors of their actions.

Some parents instill feelings of shame in their children even before they teach them to feel guilt. Shame is a more powerful and more destructive feeling than guilt. If you tell a child he/she should feel ashamed, the message generates a very uncomfortable feeling in the child and does not offer a way of getting rid of this pain. When we feel shame, we are ashamed of who we are. Shame is a feeling about the totality of oneself, i.e., one is shameful. There is no potential action that will eliminate shame. In contrast, one feels guilty about having done a *bad* thing. We can do *bad* things without being *bad* people. Furthermore, it is possible to atone for or to fix the state of affairs caused by misbehavior. In contrast, when the child has been taught to feel ashamed, no specific action or words will eliminate the shame. Shame persists whereas guilt can be dissipated. When we experience shame, we view ourselves as an unchangeable noun instead of a work in progress or a verb.

Once children have internalized the parental code of behavior as the *right* way to be, they begin to learn how to monitor and even to avoid guilty feelings. By knowing which actions are *wrong*, children can and will anticipate feeling guilty if they engage in such actions. The anticipation of feeling guilty can lead the child to choose to avoid behaviors that will generate guilt.

In fact, this is the most positive and helpful nature of guilt. If we know what will make us feel guilty, we then have the power to avoid experiencing guilt. The capacity to anticipate potential painful feelings enables us to take control over our lives. Without such anticipation, we continually find ourselves in trouble. Therefore, we need to be prone to feeling guilty so that we can take decisive action to make the right choices.

Feelings of guilt are certainly uncomfortable, but they are also quite necessary. Guilt feelings tell us that we have behaved badly and essentially function to teach us a lesson. Our guilt feelings tell us not to engage in such behavior again. It is our conscience that produces guilt feelings; and when our conscience works most efficiently, we can anticipate guilt if we were to act upon particular impulses. Our conscience can also make us feel guilty if we engage in certain behaviors we believe to be *wrong*. However, we would have fared better if we could have anticipated the guilt and thereby avoided guilt-generating activities.

When we feel guilty, we are often consumed in a process of self-punishment. We essentially function as judge and jury concerning our inappropriate behavior. However, it is very important to give yourself a fair trial rather than simply engage in excessive self-punishment. We need to make some sort of reparations to ourselves for having done the wrong thing so that we can move forward.

That is, we have to admit our wrongdoings and then promise ourselves not to repeat the mistake. Guilt feelings thereby enable us to take full and effective control over our lives.

Just as it is possible to have too little guilt, which is considered to be sociopathic, it is also possible to suffer from too much guilt. In these circumstances people are unable to forgive themselves for their wrongdoings. In both instances the unhealthy side of the personality dominates. That unhealthy side seeks to regularly inflict punishment upon the person and is quite pleased to find *proof* of bad behavior. In fact, whenever the unhealthy side of the personality becomes very strong, it regularly creates reasons to administer self-punishment. In those instances where the guilt feelings become excessive and incessant, the person soon is unable to resolve these feelings. Consequently, the feelings of guilt become transformed into depression.

The guilt feelings we experience as children are a consequence of our failure to follow the rules established by parents, religion or society at large. However, by the time children enter adolescence, they have begun to question the legitimacy of these externally imposed rules. The adolescent can defy rules for three basic reasons. Rules are first broken because following the rules means abandoning potential pleasure, and many adolescents are too pleasure-seeking to be able to systematically maintain self-control. The second reason the adolescent may break rules is the teenager simply believes these rules are wrong. The third and more complex reason is that some adolescents have a strong need to be punished. For them, guilt feelings have been twisted into a complicated form of self-attack which is generated by the unhealthy side of the personality.

Because it is common for adolescents to experience emotions in very strong or extreme degrees, many teenagers assume the position that all rules are wrong. Consequently, they rebel against externally imposed structures and morality as they strive to reach a state of personal freedom. They believe that to become your own person, you must stop automatically conforming to externally imposed standards. Therefore, many adolescents behave in similar fashion to the two-year-old child, the creature typically described as in the *terrible twos.* Many adolescents routinely say *no* and *I won't* just as the two-year-old also affirms personal power through defiance of many parental wishes.

Regularly saying *no* to everything without saying *yes* soon becomes empty and pointless behavior. Rejecting an externally imposed code of morality truly is a necessary step toward becoming one's own person. However, a second step must also take place. The adolescent needs to create a personal code of morality as a substitute for the externally imposed parental set of rules. Independent decisions on what is right and wrong for oneself is an extremely difficult task. One is likely to struggle with this task throughout life because we need to be open to changing our standards as our experiences and outlooks change.

As each of us struggles to decide upon our own personal code of morality, we are engaged in an essential reshaping of ourselves— an awesome, painful and yet wonderful process. These decisions we make on how to be and how not to be will become the new core of our being. As a result, if and when we violate this personal code of conduct, we will certainly again feel guilt, but in a more powerful way than we have ever felt guilt before. To violate one's own personal code of conduct is truly to undermine oneself.

When individuals acknowledge they have effectively established their own personal code of morality, they can feel proud of themselves. It is important to remember pride is an emotion which best remains as a personal, unverbalized feeling rather than a condition announced to others. Telling others we feel highly self-satisfied is typically an expression of arrogance rather than of pride. When you create and endorse a rigorous and demanding code of behavior, you will be pleased, feel self-satisfied and proud because you have truly taken effective control over your life. Anyone who accomplishes this has primarily overcome the unhealthy side of the personality. However, total victory is actually impossible; we still will continue to experience further personal struggle and, occasionally, guilt.

We also are all subject to a different and universal form of guilt that many people fail to acknowledge. This is called existential guilt, and it involves feeling guilty about our human limitations. We could all be better people than we have been, and we can all legitimately accuse ourselves of not having tried harder. We could all be more humanitarian and kinder to others and to our environment. We could have been more thoughtful or considerate or much more hard working. In short, everyone can be a better person which will always be true for all humans. Whenever we feel this existential guilt, it reminds us to do better or try harder and not be self-complacent. Even so, it is very difficult and sometimes impossible to comfortably say *I have done enough*. No matter what we have done, we could always have done better. We each need to find ways to come to terms with this basic truth.

Our most troubling and distressing form of guilt still is experienced whenever we specifically violate our personal code of behavior. When as children or adolescents we did not follow parental rules, we could excuse ourselves because we were not violating a personally endorsed code of ethics. However, when we fail to follow our own self chosen code of ethics, e.g., if I believe it is wrong to cheat, but nonetheless I cheat, then I must find a way to answer to myself for my misbehavior. I can be my toughest critic. Self-violations make us feel guilty, and those guilt feelings make it crucial for us to listen to the healthy side of our personality and attempt to improve ourselves. Self-monitoring and acting as judge and jury of ourselves certainly frees us from the evaluations by others but leaves us upholding the most difficult code of conduct— the code we have created for ourselves. As demanding as that code may be, it remains the best and most fulfilling way for us to lead our lives.

Passion

Earlier I discussed the dictum *I think, therefore, I am* pronounced by the French philosopher, René Descartes. This statement has had a major impact not just upon philosophy but also upon much of Western thinking as well. By placing primary importance upon thinking, Descartes stressed that we must rely upon reasoning ability in order to know things. Through this dictum Descartes asserted that logic, thinking and rationality were the central and most important qualities that defined our human condition.

Certainly our ability to think, to reason and to solve problems are major assets which enable us to cope and survive in the world. However, as stated earlier, we are also able to know things immediately through our prereflective consciousness. Our prereflective consciousness is a form of knowing that is not a consequence of reasoning. It is, quite simply, an immediate way of knowing that provides our best guideposts for living. I can categorically state as opposed to Descartes' argument, that I know I am alive because I feel alive. If I needed to resort to logic to demonstrate I was alive, I would be mistrusting my prereflective consciousness. I personally much prefer to rely upon my immediate knowing, or my prereflective consciousness, as I continue to forge my way through life.

I know what it is to be alive because I feel it with all my being. When I feel most fully alive, the best word I can use to describe that feeling is passionate. We humans can and do feel passionate about any or all aspects of living. We can feel passionate when the sun rises, the sky is blue and the air is warm and enticing. We can feel passionate upon discovering the latest book written by one of our favorite authors. We can feel passionate about the hot fudge sauce served at our favorite ice cream store. We can feel passionate about social issues and causes. We can, and hopefully do, feel passionate about the people we love. Passion means that we have very strong feelings about people, objects or events. Another way of expressing passion is to say that we deeply care. Being highly involved, or truly caring about other people or issues outside of ourselves, represents the fullest manner of experiencing. This deeply felt caring enables us to create valid and highly meaningful lives.

People typically feel most passionate during their earliest years of life. When we attend to crying babies, we notice they cry with their whole bodies. Not only do their faces grimace and turn red, but their toes curl and their bodies surge backwards and forwards. Crying is an emotion that takes over the entire infant. Babies do not simply feel happy; they are ecstatic and their entire bodies radiate with this joy. The extremely strong reactions of babies and young children are very natural because youngsters have not learned to suppress or to modulate their emotions. When the baby is hungry, hunger is all that the baby knows at that moment. Therefore, the baby is consumed with pain and screams for relief. Parents quickly learn which kind of cry is a hunger cry and are then able to satisfy the baby's need for food. Once children acquire speech, they learn to express their needs verbally rather than with screams which usually means their expressions become less passionate.

As we mature, we certainly need to learn to tone down some of our emotional expressions in order to have our needs best met. We cannot afford to express extreme emotional reactions to everything we encounter as we would be both exhausted and ineffectual. Nonetheless, it remains important to feel many things quite strongly even as we moderate some of our other reactions. One particular approach in psychology called the Gestalt school specifies that humans are psychologically most healthy when they are children because children react strongly to whatever they encounter and fully express their feelings. Gestaltists believe that far too many adults have become constricted and have severely reduced their responsiveness in emotional situations. As a result, Gestaltists say many people live bland lives. When asked to express their opinions or preferences, such adults often say it does not matter or they do not care. It might be posited that these people are engaging in some defensive or protective maneuvers by stifling their emotional expression; but a much more important and relevant description is that they have lost passion in their lives.

Some adults have not successfully learned to moderate their expressions and remain both too excessive and extreme in their emotional reactions and behavior. These individuals apparently interpret many small encounters as major and crucial events, which then enables them to justify their strong outward reactions. One such example is drivers who aggressively try to intimidate or push others off the road if they feel offended in some way. Their road rage, while certainly very immature, can unfortunately inflict significant damage upon others. Perhaps upon reflection they may realize they became too angry; but that recognition may not help when they see themselves as slighted in another situation.

When we are truly emotionally healthy, we can both love passionately and hate passionately. As with all human experiences, passion can be a wonderful and fulfilling state. It can also be very destructive if it is allowed to run amok. We do need to allow ourselves to feel passionately angry when we are violated or betrayed because such intense emotion alerts us to the fact that we must become more self-protective. Nonetheless, our intense feelings must be well enough managed so we do not become violent or lose self-control in ways we would later regret. We need to be able to express our anger in powerful ways that command respect without resorting to physical aggression. When males, in particular, progress from adolescence into adulthood, they need to learn to use words rather than fists as the best way to express anger. Far too many individuals fail to make this transition.

Not every event needs to evoke strong passion for some situations call for only a mild reaction. Being able to run the gamut of emotional reactions is very healthy because it demonstrates that we interpret life events as having different degrees of importance. Young adults often are very much in the throes of experiencing strong passionate reactions which can extend beyond the power of sexual attraction. What is especially wonderful about being a young adult is that along with strong passionate feelings, there is often a concomitant expansion of awareness of self and others. When young adults are heavily engaged in questioning and discovering their own place in the world, their passion, expressed through the prereflective consciousness, will help them find the best directions to pursue.

Being passionate remains a key for healthy living as an individual matures and passes through different stages of adulthood. If one settles into a repetitive living pattern which stifles new interests or personal gratifications, it becomes very easy to fall into depression. As adults we certainly experience excessive time demands from our jobs and from our children. Often we have heavy financial pressures and major difficulties dealing with our own aging parents. Nonetheless, we need to keep ourselves attuned to positive and inviting aspects of living in order to keep us feeling passionately alive.

No human being will ever have the wisdom to be passionate only in healthy ways. However, we are blessed with the capacity to reflect upon our past behaviors and to learn from our blunders. Whenever our passions have led us in the wrong direction, we can introspect and discover when and where we needed to use stronger controls. At other times, self-reflection can tell us that a strong, passionate reaction was a wonderful experience — absolutely right for the moment and for the situation. If we do not reflect upon and evaluate our past behaviors, then our passions will certainly lead us into trouble. Without reflection, there cannot be self-control; and without self-control, we lose the essential capacity to become better and more fulfilled people.

We need to be able to follow the knowing and feeling experiences produced by our prereflective consciousness. Occasionally we will take missteps in following our feelings. However, we can then use introspection to better understand and change ourselves. The *knowing* of prereflective consciousness regularly guides our behavior. We would truly be lost if we stopped trusting this *knowing* and tried to rely upon logic before taking any action. The trusting of the prereflective consciousness is what leads us to *being plumb.* The pursuit of passions is often the wise knowing of *being plumb*—fully knowing and following what is right for each of us.

One cannot find an easy and predictable path toward greater self-fulfilment. Too much self-analysis can turn us into overly intellectualized beings preoccupied with the wonder of our own navels. On the other hand, too little self-reflection leaves us functioning impulsively and often behaving in an obnoxious, inconsiderate manner. One general guidepost may be followed concerning self-reflection and insight. When a situation works out well, we rarely engage in introspection. In those situations we learn to increase our level of self-trust. It is only when our actions lead to unhappy or painful results that self-analysis is called for. Such self-questioning helps us better understand what went wrong and how to respond better in a similar situation.

In young adulthood most of us fully express our passions in ways that produce much personal growth. It is perhaps easiest to follow one's passion in late adolescence when we are not hampered by many external responsibilities. Consequently, many college students travel to youth hostels or take summer courses in foreign lands. One's late teens and early 20s is certainly an ideal time to engage in passionate love affairs and to feel deeply about issues and causes. If one does not sign petitions or go to demonstrations at age 20, it is unlikely that person will be socially concerned upon reaching 40.

The fullest level of participation in life is expressed through deep caring. Such caring begins by opening up oneself to full experiencing. However, for many young adults, the wish to expand experience becomes focused upon finding a *high* through drugs or alcohol. These experiences are essentially self-centered ways of feeling with no focus upon issues or others. Too many people want to change what they are feeling and experiencing, but they are not invested in wanting to change themselves.

Consequently, using drugs and alcohol is often similar to the use of prescribed medications designed to change feelings or emotions. However, the best kind of *high* one can experience is to be passionately involved with life, a quest that can be the most fulfilling.

Even when the individual does not find healthy self-expression, passion and self-direction in the early stages of adulthood, a new opportunity for further growth will arise in the mid-life years. At that time individuals are even more likely to question themselves and the direction of their lives as they seek greater fulfilment. The best road for such self-discovery includes the ability to be passionate.

Again, what we each ultimately need is to find a balance between being fully passionate and being very sensible. We must retain the power of our emotions for that is the legacy of our animal history. More than that, we need to live our lives as fully as possible, and by doing so we are expressing and developing our individuality. We need to temper these passions with reason, so that sometimes we follow our passions and other times we follow our reason. In this way we remain an interesting combination of the best of all worlds. It requires juggling, but change keeps life interesting. We are, after all, only processes; and as processes we will change over time.

Certainly it is vital that we allow ourselves to remain passionate human beings, but we need to deal with each specific passion quite differently. In particular we need to find effective ways of expressing anger, which is probably the most troublesome human emotion. We also need to find effective and fulfilling ways of expressing love. Each of these emotions is so important that they will be addressed in separate chapters.

Anger

Virtually all humans feel angry at some point in their lives. Some could be correctly characterized as generally angry individuals while others rarely experience anger. For most people, anger is part of their repertoire of experiences, yet many individuals are very uncomfortable with this emotion. I use the word "anger" to cover a wide gamut of negative feelings which range from being mildly annoyed to experiencing either a hot or a cold rage. Feeling angry is a natural component of our humanness. Being able to comfortably express our anger is considered a healthy human quality as long as the expression does not become abusive, violent or transformed into rage.

Earlier in the text I referred to the human dilemma of existing as both a subject (in control of one's life) and an object (victimized by external forces). We are most likely to feel anger whenever we are treated as an object, especially when others ignore our needs. To feel angry because we are treated like an object is one way to reconnect with our sense of ourselves as subjects. We need and want to demonstrate that we are not simply objects. We have personal power and desire to exercise that power at those times when others disregard us.

Even though it is positive and healthy to feel angry when we are mistreated, all too often the expression of anger comes from the unhealthy side of our personality. Whenever anger is excessive, has negative consequences or boomerangs against the angry person, it is because the unhealthy side has temporarily taken control. Most of us have experienced these small lapses of control. These are the moments in an argument when one *goes too far* and says hurtful things that cannot be retracted. The unhealthy side of the personality has done the speaking for us. In such situations, a simple and direct statement of our anger would have come from the healthy part of the personality. Once we cross the line and become particularly hurtful, it is our unhealthy side which has temporarily taken control.

Whenever we first feel angry, our unhealthy side is offered a perfect opportunity to steer us in the wrong or ultimately self-destructive direction. It is important to remember that our unhealthy side uses the same wise brain as does our healthy side, and these unhealthy tendencies can keep fueling our anger by telling us we are justified in being furious. It can find incident after incident to stoke the fires of our anger until we are simply consumed by these very hostile feelings. By the time the unhealthy side has completed advocating its case, a minor situation can become transformed into what appears to be a life and death situation. As a result, self-awareness is especially necessary whenever we experience angry feelings. With self-monitoring we become most able to behave out of our healthy side. Anger is a very complicated emotion that can be aroused by many different events. It can also be used to cover up other feelings and issues. Therefore, it is very important that we understand its sources and values, as well as the potential danger of showing anger.

One of the first principles psychologists discovered about anger was that frustration frequently leads to aggression. Very young children easily become angry whenever they do not get what they want. The anger expressed by the infant and small child represents the child's first expression of power. Children express their anger by yelling, grabbing, pushing, biting or countless other strategies designed to get their own way. By expressing these angry feelings, children transform themselves from feeling powerless into feeling powerful.

In some home situations, children quickly learn it is too dangerous for them to express their anger. Whatever anger they did express was met by even more powerful expressions of frightening anger from the parental figures. In families where the expression of anger by a child is met with such fury, the child finds it so dangerous to be angry that she/he stops being aware of the anger. Other children learn that the expression of their anger is indeed a very powerful tool. By throwing temper tantrums, they get their parents to bend to their will and give them whatever they want. These two simple examples demonstrate that in our early home environment we learn when, if and how to express our anger.

Because the expression of anger is an expression of power, the targets of our anger rarely encourage us to express our power directly toward them. Parents may encourage expressing anger toward other people, but they are unlikely to encourage such expressions toward themselves. This is just one example of the many ways we receive contradictory messages about being angry. Most children are taught the biblical injunction which states *Thou shalt not kill*, yet if they turn on the television or play computer games or go to the movies, they see that killing is both sanctioned and rampant. Even more importantly, children quickly discover we live in a society which creates armies, wages war, drops bombs and considers such behavior morally justified.

The contradiction between expressing and stifling one's anger is also revealed in the different messages of the biblical Old and New Testaments. The Old Testament advocates *An eye for an eye and a tooth for a tooth* whereas the New Testament advocates *Turn the other cheek*. Children are given the messages that it is bad to be angry and also it is good to be angry. They ultimately must independently decide when, how and why to express that anger.

As children mature, they develop a general sense of *what should and should not be*. They come to believe how other people ought to behave both generally and toward them in particular. We expect other people to engage in certain behaviors and conduct their lives in specific ways.

When the other person does not behave in the ways they *should*, we often expect them to stop because what they have been doing is *wrong*. Sometimes we expect or even demand that others apologize for their actions. The first experiences that lead us to anger are the specific expectations or demands we hold for other people.

A second component leading to our anger is when we are convinced we are entitled to have the other person satisfy our expectations. Entitlement is a higher level concept that would seem to be above the grasp of a two-year-old. However, when we see a toddler scream *MINE* and take a swat at a sibling or even a parent, we can easily recognize that even young children believe they should get what they want. As we mature, our relationships with others become far more complicated. By the time we reach adulthood, we often have many complex expectations of others existing alongside our strong feelings of entitlement. People who have strong beliefs about what they are entitled to will have frequent bouts of anger; they feel it is perfectly within their rights to demand others comply with their wishes. On the other hand, those who lack a strong sense of entitlement will be far less prone to experience anger. One of the ways unentitled people may express angry feelings is by focusing upon larger social issues. They may feel righteous indignation for particular social policies or governmental actions rather than allowing themselves to feel angry about personal treatment.

The final component leading to expression of anger is the need to assert our personal power. We tell others we are angry because our intention is to make them change their behavior. Assuming a moral high ground, we want them to stop doing what is *wrong* and start doing what is *right*. However, close inspection of our own overt behavior, *anger*, casts serious doubt on that supposed moral stance. In such instances, it usually is the unhealthy side of the personality which directs our behavior. Often people who feel wronged by others take the position–*I will teach him*. Of course, these individuals do not teach anything other than the "teacher" has an anger problem.

Any expression of anger always contains at least an implicit expression of power. By letting the other person know we are angry with either what they have or have not done, we inform them of what we will or will not tolerate. In such instances, expressing one's anger is affirming one's self. This message is setting limits with other people. It says they will not be allowed to take advantage of or hurt us again. For example, if you are to meet someone at 7:00 and they do not show up until 8:30, you would first expect an explanation for their tardiness. If they fail to apologize or explain their lateness, it will be effectively self-assertive as well as important to let them know you are angry and will not again tolerate such behavior. If you fail to give the other person that message, you are implicitly telling him/her not to respect you. Therefore, you will likely be mistreated by that person in the future.

By now it should be readily apparent that I am not a strong believer in routinely *turning the other cheek*. I do not see any sense in forgiving someone who neither asks for forgiveness nor tries to atone for errors or hurtful behavior. If you simply forgive a person who does not even admit to having engaged in wrongdoing, it seems obvious you are giving him/her license to repeat the offensive behavior. It is wise and rational to accept apologies and to mend fences; however, it is not wise to perpetuate the role of victim. It is healthy to directly express our anger in specific situations, particularly when we have good reasons for so doing.

When another person treats us *wrongly,* it is an important cue to take immediate action. The best action here is some form of self-assertion. It is usually most productive to express dissatisfaction with the other person's behavior as soon as you feel annoyed. If you quickly express dissatisfaction, you will not have time to ruminate over any past supposedly wrong treatment and escalate your emotions into stronger feelings of anger. The more immediately we express ourselves, the easier it is for the other person to make the necessary concessions. Once anger has been allowed to escalate, it becomes a tool of our unhealthy side. At that time, you will be too angry for the other person to want to make any concessions. An attempt to intimidate the other person makes them angry, which makes ultimate reconciliation very difficult.

When we feel annoyed but fail to speak out, our anger will escalate and reach a point where it is too strong to be directly expressed. The longer you hold onto angry feelings without giving them direct expression, the more uncomfortable you will feel. Unexpressed anger destroys relationships. In such situations the angry person continues to seethe and soon will feel no desire to fix the relationship.

When we use self-assertion effectively, problems are less likely to escalate. By expressing expectations clearly, you can have a discussion or an argument over specific issues without personalizing or inflating the problem into major proportions. On the other hand, when a friend presents you with a list of grievances compiled over the past months or years, it is apparent that this "friend" regularly cherishes feelings of anger without allowing a direct resolution to the problem. These individuals extensively nurse their grievances until their sense of righteous indignation prevents any positive resolutions.

Individuals uncomfortable in expressing anger often use rationalizations to cover up this discomfort. Some non-assertive people deceive themselves into believing the actions of others do not make them angry. They often say they themselves are *nice* and do not want to be *petty*. One can use a sense of morality to justify both the expression as well as the non-expression of anger.

Anger is one of the strongest ways to express power. Therefore, some people frequently compensate for their lack of felt power by expressing anger in *safe* situations. A person who feels oppressed at work may take it out on the family pet or family members. If such behavior regularly persists or becomes abusive, the perpetrator obviously has serious anger management problems and requires outside intervention. Some people may use their car and driving to feel powerful over others because they cannot find a way to be effectively powerful in their personal lives. Different examples demonstrate how the unhealthy side of the personality can take over the expression of anger. Indeed, anger is an emotion that often functions as a magnet for the appearance of the unhealthy side of the personality.

Physically and emotionally abusive people operate out of the unhealthy side of their personality. They regularly express anger in order to feel powerful. It is not likely they will voluntarily engage in self-exploration or attempt to understand and eliminate horrific behavior. Changing this behavior would mean abandonment of the primary way of feeling powerful. Most of these individuals implicitly feel such a change would be too costly and humiliating.

Too many of us have been badly damaged by the hostility of others, be it by strangers or family members. When we have been beaten, sexually violated or traumatized in different ways by these violent people, no form of limit-setting or expression of anger can make our hurt disappear. Our anger at these perpetrators need not disappear, but we cannot let it dominate our existence. If it does so, we need to seek professional assistance to become released from this dominant pain.

If you have been spared such trauma, you will find that setting healthy limits in a direct manner is a valuable strategy for successful living. In order to effectively set limits, it is important to be insightful or self-reflective. Nonetheless, we must also remember that others, just like ourselves, are fallible humans who will continue to make mistakes. If we act *holier than thou*, we set ourselves up for disappointment and trouble in relationships. We all need to understand and carefully study the ways in which our unhealthy side operates. We also need to be aware of the power of our healthy side so we can draw upon it to exert effective control of our lives.

Anger is a necessary and wonderful tool to use in effective living, but it can be a terrible weapon in the hands of the unhealthy side of the personality. The better we know ourselves, the more we will choose to live by drawing upon the wisdom and knowledge of our healthy side.

Lust and Love

I decided to discuss lust and love immediately after writing about anger because far too often, sexual acts have become mechanisms for expressing anger or even hatred toward others. We live in a society whose most popular curse is to say "fuck you" to whomever has made us angry. When we were children and first heard this phrase, most of us readily understood it described anger and hatred. We knew that we were hearing an expression of anger even though most of us did not yet know what the word "fuck" meant.

Both men and women have found countless ways to turn sexuality into either a direct or an indirect expression of anger. The most blatant expression of such anger or hostility is through rape, and the individual who commits rape is expressing rage rather than lust. It is a historical fact that conquering armies often raped the women of the subjugated country. Unfortunately, that form of violence is still currently repeated, most notably in the recent Bosnian conflict where women of either side were regularly raped by the opposing troops. However, rape is no longer the harshest example of how sexual activity can be used to express extreme hostility toward another.

The prevalence of many sexually transmitted diseases, including the potentially life-ending AIDS virus, places all individuals who engage in unprotected sex at risk of disease and death. People who know they carry such transmittable diseases but continue to engage in unprotected sex are attempting to hurt, maim and even kill their sexual partners. Some may not be willing to directly admit to their hostility; but it is nonetheless true that they are expressing an extraordinarily high level of aggression to another.

At this worst extreme, sexual behavior is a vehicle used to express destructive emotions. However, sexual behavior can also be a vehicle for expressing a host of other wishes. Sexual activity can be used to directly or indirectly express other feelings, and it can be used to convey a range of positive as well as negative emotions.

At the highest level of psychological health, sexual participation is used to express the deep and mutual love between two people. Here the sexual act does not simply give vent to lustful feelings; it also serves as a vehicle for the expression of commitment and caring. Because sexual behavior is usually an activity involving two people, it is important that both acknowledge the personhood of their sexual partner and, at least, treat that person with respect. If one fails to do so, then the other participant is viewed simply as a sexual object without the full complement of human needs and emotions.

Even if both participants wish to approach sexual activity for purposes of mutual enjoyment, it is extremely difficult simply to be sexual with no other meaning for the behavior. People cannot fully separate their sexuality from the rest of their being. Consequently, whatever we do sexually reflects upon who we are and what we believe in. Whenever we wish to engage in sexual activity, we first need to find or be in a relationship with another person who is willing to accommodate our needs. It is only the narcissistic and hate-filled people who force their will onto others and, thereby, commit rape. For the rest of us of both sexes, when we want to achieve sexual pleasure, we need to find another who is willing to provide us with satisfaction. Because the sexual act requires at least some sort of accommodation, sexual situations are ripe for the expression of personal power.

Many men in particular view sexual activity as a way of demonstrating their power or machismo. Because western culture has too often equated sex with power instead of with love, many individuals find themselves unable to simply and easily love their partners. Adler (1968) observed that our society has typically equated masculinity with superiority and femininity with inferiority. Sexuality often becomes the primary arena where men attempt to demonstrate their power over women by subjugating them into an inferior role. Many women understandably reject this kind of treatment and try to attain a more superior role through many different methods.

Whenever sexuality becomes an arena for the expression of personal power, underlying and at times overt conflict develops between the two individuals. For this reason the label of "castrating" has often been given to women who are not generally meek and compliant. The phrase obviously was created by males. The castration is symbolic and only could occur when a man defines his masculinity by the degree of power held over a woman. Any man who thinks this would most likely try to reassert his power whenever he felt it was challenged by a woman. One of the best classic and humorous examples of such expressions of power was routinely demonstrated in the old, popular TV program *The Honeymooners.* The Jackie Gleason character, Ralph, would frequently make a fist and warn his wife *Alice, how would you like a trip to the moon*? This gesture and comment were his way of putting Alice back in her "proper" place.

Nonetheless, wherever a basic power struggle exists between a man and woman, it is likely that the woman put in the inferior role will try to alter the balance of power. Some females are often able to take away the males' sense of power and potency by refusing to engage in intercourse by claiming fatigue, a headache or various other maladies. People of either sex who engage in such power games not only punish their partners by such activities but also deprive themselves of sexual gratification.

Either a man or woman can view the sexual act as only a mechanism for sexual pleasure and, consequently, regard the partner simply as an object of potential pleasure. It has historically been more common for males to seek sexual gratification from a partner and look for nothing more. In order for men to be able to satisfy these lustful drives, prostitution has been customary for much of the course of civilization. Of course, many men desire far more from a bed partner than achieving simple sexual release. However, it is more prevalent for a woman to seek more from the man than just sexual pleasure. Most women want to be treated with affection and hope to be loved by their sexual partner. It is these wishes, too often unfulfilled, along with misdirected fantasies, that often lead the woman into bed with a man.

As a result, the most common complaint couples bring into marital therapy is that the man believes he gets too little sex and the woman believes she gets too little affection. The behaviorally-oriented marital therapist might create a reward system to solve this problem whereby the male is issued tokens by the woman for each overt sign of affection displayed toward her. Such activities could include buying flowers or candy, holding hands, saying affectionate things, etc. Whenever the male attains a sufficient number of tokens, they can be traded in for an evening of sexual intercourse. A male who participates in such counseling hopefully will learn to express this affection spontaneously and persist with it over time, which should strengthen the relationship. Even though such a simple strategy often works, it unfortunately re-enacts the sexual power struggle, albeit at a somewhat higher level.

The person who primarily seeks an attractive sex object to achieve gratification is functioning at the aesthetic level, a concept of Kierkegaard's discussed earlier.

Such a person is not capable of love unless he/she exerts a strong act of will to create personal change. The sexual partner of such an aesthete, who erroneously sees their mate as loving, has created a fantasy world to compensate for painful reality. This wishful individual is likely also to remain unfulfilled in the real world, using denial and fantasy as a means of coping.

These problematic behaviors have been present for centuries, certainly predating the sexual revolution of 40 years ago. Notwithstanding, important widespread changes in sexual attitudes and behavior have occurred because of social changes during the 60s. That was a decade of extreme rebellion by adolescents and young adults. They broke long-standing sexual taboos as they practiced free love, formed and joined communes and created the motto *Make love, not war.* Sexual taboos were discarded, and many people also ceased to view authority figures as indisputable experts. There were demonstrations against police who were mockingly labeled *pigs*, as well as massive anti-war protests in Washington, DC. Organized religion as well lost some ability to lead congregants as young adults became mistrustful of everyone who was not rebelling. Drug experimentation was quite common and, unfortunately, remains far too prevalent today.

Before the sexual revolution, many people, especially females, were inhibited when it came to expressing their sexual needs. Although unwed couples did not typically remain celibate, they usually deferred sexual intercourse until they had made a significant commitment with each other. Of course, some individuals found easy outlets for sexual expression even though it was often viewed as a form of slumming. Many men paid for the services of prostitutes or sought out women considered to have low standards. Most women were usually very cautious before they became intimate with a man because such behavior could ruin their reputations. That form of social condemnation is long known and perhaps best documented in Nathaniel Hawthorne's 1850 novel, *The Scarlet Letter.* For many centuries among the upper economic classes, including royalty, it was common for powerful men to have charming and intelligent mistresses. Attractive women who entered these relationships acquired status, power and wealth in exchange for sexual favors. Such women today are designated as "trophy wives."

Prior to the sexual revolution, individuals engaged in sexual activity either for basic gratification (what can be called lust), or they used sexuality and intercourse as a way of expressing their intimate feelings (or love) for one another. In the first half of the 20th century, mental health professionals viewed individuals who had difficulty expressing their sexual urges as frightened of becoming intimate with others. The changed atmosphere of the 60s made it much easier for most people to become routinely sexual; and, consequently, fewer people needed therapy to help them be sexually liberated.

Many people today still casually engage in uninhibited sexual intercourse; unfortunately, the behavior often extends to youngsters who are still of middle school age. I too frequently hear about twelve-year-old children engaging in oral sex, justifying their actions by saying it is not sex because the former President said so. Certainly, it is healthier for young adults and older adolescents to be able to fulfill their sexual needs rather than to be dominated by inhibitions and guilt. However, sense and sensibility need to be used to temper the power of lust.

The legacy of the 60s was an elimination of taboos against engaging in casual sex. Now if an individual has no sexual inhibitions, he/she is left with the basic questions of choosing what to do and what not to do. In other words, now sexual activity is not necessarily wrong — nor is it necessarily right. Decisions on sexual activity have to be independently made just as one must make personal decisions about all other potential activities.

Whenever you engage in sexual activity with a casual acquaintance, you need to acknowledge that you are satisfying underlying feelings of lust. To experience the desire for basic sexual pleasure is to feel lust. In order to gratify our lust, we seek out objects that will provide us with sexual release or gratification. When we are driven by lust, we are not really interested in the person we go to bed with. What we simply want at such times is to find an attractive person who can both arouse us and give us pleasure. In the absence of another person, sometimes our lustful feelings demand we treat ourselves as sexual objects and engage in masturbation. Our biology is responsible for those lustful feelings, which means that experiencing strong sexual feelings is simply a natural part of our humanness. How and if and when we decide to satisfy those lustful feelings is essentially a matter of personal choice. The particular sexual choices made, just as all other choices, are expressions of one's humanness. These choices represent the ways in which you continue to express and to recreate yourself.

There are times when the need for sexual satisfaction is so strong that the object used for gratification matters very little. The sexual revolution openly allowed females to join males in the simple pursuit of sexual pleasure. Throughout adolescence and young adulthood, hormones are very strong, and the need for sexual gratification is very powerful. The still-present machismo in males was documented in the lyrics of a popular song a few years ago that proclaimed *the girls all looked prettier at closing time.* We all have lustful feelings. Even in the closest intimate and loving relationships, at times we simply want to experience sexual release and gratification. We are not always interested in love making; sometimes all we want is sexual pleasure.

It is also important to acknowledge that we live in a country obsessed with sexuality. The media in our society has long recognized that sex sells. Consequently, advertising and the entertainment industry use sex to sell their products. Most people, though more women than men, are so inundated with sexual messages that some of them believe it is imperative to make themselves as attractive as possible. Insecure people often try to reshape themselves physically so that they are seen as sexually desirable, so they engage in fanatical exercise and diets. Enormous energies are used in the attempt to be perfect physical specimens. But even with compliments on appearance, the physically attractive people realize it is only the physical body that is found desirable. Accordingly, it is the outer self that is lusted for and the inner self which is often ignored.

Our natural lustful feelings coupled with the media message proclaiming the importance of sexuality has led many people to believe it is their basic right to be regularly sexually gratified. A preoccupation with finding diverse sexual pleasures is one of the prime reasons that over half the married people in our country commit adultery. The need to satisfy feelings of lust is quite powerful; but we are all quite capable of deferring sexual pleasure. When we are promiscuous, we are expressing base animal instincts rather than affirming our human capacity to make meaningful choices.

The confusion of sex and power has also led to sexual performance problems in some males. These men are so focused upon performing, or demonstrating their male dominance, that they become unable to respond to the immediacy of the other person. In other words, they are so self-focused that they treat sexuality as a one person operation, which will be doomed to failure. Anxiety about sexuality, just as anxiety about any other topic, can seriously interfere with the individual's functioning. When we allow ourselves simply to "be" with the other person, in a physical as well as a psychological sense, there will be no problems with sexual adequacy. However, some individuals view sexuality as an Olympic sport with a rating for level of performance. They will deserve no better than low or failing marks because they have lost the real intimacy of the encounter.

Perhaps the most destructive consequence of our societal sexual preoccupation is that many people believe they cannot be liked or loved if they reveal their inner selves. In other words, they are afraid to express their ideas, wishes or insecurities because they believe that is not what other people want to hear or know. Instead they carefully try to present a positive facade. If indeed they receive positive responses to this facade, they may very slowly reveal small pieces of themselves to check for possible reactions. Unfortunately, the person who is likely to be attracted to the facade is also very unlikely to be attracted to the real person underneath. Consequently, such a behavioral strategy is frequently likely to fail.

Most people basically want to be loved for themselves, but too many do not trust this will happen. Individuals are willing to settle for quick sexual pleasure and move from partner to partner in order to obtain more gratification. It does feel good to be sexually gratified, but it becomes an empty feeling over time because most of us wish to experience something more than immediate physical pleasure.

To have loving feelings toward another is to respond to the whole person rather than to a sexual object. In love we value the other. In caring for another, we want both to protect them and help them grow and develop. This core aspect of love does not necessarily have a sexual component. It can be the love of a parent for a child, or the love of a sibling for a sibling, or the love of a friend for a friend.

When sexual urges are an added component to the deep caring for another, we reach the most gratifying level of human relationships. When our love is reciprocated, it is the most wonderful feeling in the world. However when the loved one does not reciprocate, we experience pain. When we love a partner, we are also affirming ourselves by expressing our caring for the other person. In return, we hope to find ourselves understood, cared for and also affirmed. Such love requires the intimate sharing of oneself that goes beyond the blending of bodies. To attain such a deep love requires a risk of being fully open about ourselves and a willingness to risk criticism and even possible rejection.

During adolescence and young adulthood, most of us fall in love for the first time. Often that strong passion leads us to believe that we have found our lifetime soul mate. Unfortunately this is rarely true. As adolescents and young adults our attitudes, values and interests often change in radical ways. It is common for both individuals to naturally grow apart, for both need to develop as independent people. When these adolescent relationships fail, we feel terrible pain and loss. Many people protect themselves against such future pain by maintaining emotional distance from others. Being deeply hurt once seems to be one time too many.

Many people are terrified of engaging in the intimacy that healthy love demands. They are very willing to share their bodies but not their souls. The first and most basic reason for such fear is that when you open yourself to real intimacy, you also make yourself vulnerable. Ironically, we can only be vulnerable if we have a strong enough sense of ourselves to know we can survive, even if the relationship ends. Insecure people with a weak sense of self cannot take such a risk.

When we do risk loving and being intimate, the rewards are incredible. When one of my therapy clients fell in love, his descriptions led me to believe he was participating in a very healthy form of mutual love. As a result of feeling the validation and deep caring from this woman, my client made very rapid progress in his personal therapy. That level of caring was crucial in leading him to better psychological health, and it certainly made my job as a therapist much easier. Love is extraordinarily powerful. The gift of such love makes it much easier for us to take risks and be willing to grow in ways we never before thought possible.

For each of us there will be times when we know it is right for us to relax our defenses, to risk loving and allowing ourselves to be loved. At those times we *know* this is the right decision. Those moments, of which we can always be particularly proud, are the times when we are most definitely *being plumb.* Taking risks is a necessary part of *being plumb*, especially when it comes to love. However, before we can discuss the right kinds of necessary risks, we need to first address the wrong kind or the unnecessary risks we humans take.

NECESSARY RISK TAKING

Whenever one takes a significant risk, it is quite common to experience an adrenalin rush, as the body prepares a fight or flight reaction. It has been long considered a sign of machismo for a male to deliberately place himself in a situation where he is physically challenged or at risk, and for him to emerge as master of the situation. Playing games of *chicken* with an automobile, showing that one can hold more liquor than the next person, and refusing to back down from a fight are all activities that hold a significant amount of risk. To emerge victorious in any of these activities may temporarily give the person a heightened sense of self-esteem. However, the individual who continues to engage in such confrontations will inevitably face another who will prove more powerful; therefore, his self-esteem will most likely suffer.

In a few situations it is rational and important to place one's physical safety at risk. People who work in fire and police departments accept the necessity of placing their lives at risk, for it is a built-in part of the job. A person may jump in front of a speeding car to save a small child's life. However for the most part, rarely must we take risks with our physical beings.

It is far more necessary for us to deliberately place our emotional and psychological beings at risk as part of moving forward with our lives. Older people are more likely to accept this truth than are most younger adults and adolescents. Because "we have been around the block a few times," older adults have endured many emotional pains which have taught us that we are indeed survivors. We have lived through failed relationships and failed jobs and know we can overcome whatever traumas may lurk around the corner.

Most adults have not only survived emotional traumas but have also experienced the joy of successfully reaching out and deeply connecting with other people. They may be more willing to continue the risk of potential rejections because in the past they have been successful in attempts to get close to another person. Experience can and often does provide perspective and comfort, which is quite reassuring. The late adolescent or young adult does not have this large backlog of emotional successes and failures to rely upon. Often the young adult feels too threatened to allow her/himself to be needy and vulnerable.

Young adults feel deeply passionate about many things. They love and rage deeply and often are unable to diminish the strength of their different feelings. As a result, young adults know all too well that the risks in the emotional realm are extremely threatening. To break up with your first love, to risk rejection through reaching out, to deliberately change locales and friends when departing for college all can be experiences fraught with terror. Most young adults primarily feel their vulnerability in their emotional realm, while older adults are more particularly concerned with their physical vulnerability. All of us, irrespective of age or sex, will always be vulnerable in both the physical and emotional realms. We each have to decide when to either increase or decrease that level of vulnerability.

Males as well as females must be able to take the necessary risks with their emotional lives so they can continue to grow and develop. We are all works in progress. Change is natural, and we will feel anxious whenever we consider making any significant changes in our lives. We move forward in self-development only when we are willing to take risks. If we refuse to open ourselves up to making significant life changes, we are likely to stagnate.

What we regularly must put at risk are the feelings of security we possess at any particular moment. We know what each current situation holds for us, and we know who and how we are at that particular time. If we are not in an especially satisfying relationship, we still are able to draw some comfort from knowing what the relationship does and does not provide. If we decide to step out of the relationship or to end it, then we lose whatever sense of security that relationship provided. The old adage *The devil you know is preferable to the devil that you do not know* is lived out repeatedly in the choices that many people continue to make.

To risk change is to leap willingly into an abyss where security disappears. We give up the familiar for what we hope will be something much better. We must have a certain level of underlying self-confidence in order to take such risks. People who felt fully loved as children are those most able to take chances and risk rejection. They know their personal value because it has been affirmed by others; and, consequently, they can trust that others will love and appreciate them. Nonetheless, making important choices is still fraught with anxiety for them because it involves a leap into the unknown. It requires courage to take such risks.

Relinquishing safety is very uncomfortable, especially when no other place or person is available to provide a sense of comfort. However, if you continue a deficient relationship and refuse to embrace change, you will restrict your life in unnecessary ways. For example, few people have been able to sustain their first adolescent love affair over the course of a lifetime. It is quite unusual for two people to be able to develop in parallel and complementary ways as they move from ages 16 to 60. Typically we lose our elementary and high school friends and sometimes even our college friends as we move forward with our lives. It is a very special gift to be able to sustain a deep friendship from childhood into late adulthood.

For those of us not deeply affirmed or loved by parental figures, it is far more difficult to be able to trust in oneself and others and thereby take significant life risks. Many people unhappy in their marriages will take steps to divorce only when they have a new lover in hand. Without knowing what the future holds, many people opt to retain the familiar even when it is unsatisfying. Countless others do not even consider the possibility of making any major life choices despite high levels of unhappiness. Because they feel they are unlovable and unworthy, they believe to initiate changes would only make their lives more painful.

We all know someone who appears to be stunted in emotional growth. He/she continues to behave like a teenager even into late middle age. These people sense that assuming a more adult stance will only lead to failure, so they continue to act as adolescents. It takes high levels of courage to make important changes in one's life; but when people muster such courage, they ultimately realize that making such choices were among the proudest moments of their lives.

In my life work as a therapist, I have had clients who struggled to recreate themselves by leaving destructive relationships, risking increased isolation. I found these individuals quite admirable and indeed lovable because they fought to undo the personal damage inflicted in both their early and current relationships. It is far easier to make important life changes when one has a background and history of security than after a lifetime of personal abuse and rejection.

When we do let ourselves risk rejection and make significant life changes, either by entering or leaving intimate relationships, we ultimately are able to see that the enormous risks we took were wise, even if the new relationship fails. This point was beautifully made by Viktor Frankl (1960) when he posed the question *If you could wipe away all your unhappy love affairs so that they would never have been, would you?* In raising this question, Frankl wanted his readers to recognize that suffering gives life meaning; we can take solace and also grow through our failed relationships.

Because we are human, we are flawed and will do silly and stupid things as we proceed through life. Of course we will do wonderful and admirable things as well. Mistakes can be important lessons. We need to forgive ourselves for our mistakes so that we can learn from them in the future. We cannot allow the unhealthy side of our personality to gain dominance and continually punish us for these errors.

One of the most wonderful developments I have witnessed over the course of my lifetime is that people are living much longer. Greater longevity has made it possible for individuals to take more time before settling down into at least semi-permanent life roles. It is now rare, instead of typical, for people to marry at the end of four years of college. In fact, most people now take longer than four years to complete a bachelor's degree. In a comparable vein, many young adults spend several years after college at an assortment of jobs and in a series of different relationships. All of these experiences help people to discover what (and who) is basically most satisfying and fulfilling. Being able to live longer makes it less urgent for people in their 20s to find the key paths for living.

Changes in the workplace and in the hiring processes of large corporations have made it mandatory for people to be able to reinvent themselves by acquiring different job skills. It is expected for most adults to have at least six major jobs over the course of a lifetime, and they must prepare themselves to be able to make such changes. Today is a very different kind of world from that of my youth, for the job security that was present in past decades no longer exists. For example, I received tenure in a university after only six years of teaching, and I remained in that position for 35 years; I believe that would be impossible for a new professor today. Likewise, corporations once hired people for a lifetime, and now employees can routinely expect to be fired at a moment's notice.

It is important to review these few truths because it shows the necessity of taking significant risks in our lives. We must recognize that we are social beings who need to be affirmed and loved by other people. We can receive the most important validation from others and from the person with whom we have our most intimate relationship. We need to be fully known which only is possible when we dare to share the unattractive parts of us. To be loved as a fallible human being is the greatest gift anyone can ever be given. However, you cannot receive such love unless you are willing to risk sharing yourself. Furthermore, your willingness to love another person fully and unconditionally is one of the strongest and deepest ways you can affirm yourself. If the other person fails to accept and love you for who you are, then you know it is wise to leave the relationship; and you should leave quickly. When we leave the unsatisfying relationship, we offer ourselves the opportunity of finding a person who will truly affirm us. We can really know—this is the right person—when we have learned to trust in ourselves and in our ability to *be plumb*.

Unnecessary Risk Taking

People can expose themselves to either or both types of unnecessary risks. We can place our physical being at risk, and we can place our emotional being at risk. It traditionally is more common for males to take unnecessary physical risks and for females to take unnecessary emotional risks. Of course, there are many exceptions to this generalization, for many women also may take unnecessary physical risks, and numerous males will take unnecessary emotional risks as do many women. Nonetheless, for purposes of discussion it is easier to describe these forms of risk taking along gender lines.

Because I am not young, I have acquired a different perspective on taking risks than the position I held as an adolescent and young adult. I have undergone a diverse number of life experiences which, I believe, have afforded me a certain degree of wisdom I did not possess when I was younger. It would indeed be tragic if I had learned nothing from my experiences, for one should at least become somewhat wiser through the process of aging.

One significant way in which my views have changed concerns the risks that I now consider to be worth taking *vs* those that I deem unnecessary and dangerous. Like most older adults in that regard, we label many more behavior patterns as unnecessary risk taking than will younger people. However, I believe this is primarily due to the fact that we are more realistic rather than because we are generally more afraid of danger.

Placing one's physical being at risk is a very common practice among male adolescents and young adults. The young adult usually possesses boundless energy, vitality and power. The 20-year-old can stay up all night and still function well the next day. Also, young adults have extraordinarily fast reaction times which is readily apparent when physically competing with someone 10 or 15 years older. On the tennis court, the 18-year-old can easily retrieve balls an older opponent would not even consider chasing. On the occasions when young adults actually become injured, their bodies heal so quickly they can easily believe themselves capable of withstanding and surviving anything.

This sense of boundless power is a wonderful attribute of the young adult. It is, in part, responsible for believing they can change the world; and this idealism has fueled many different social movements. Most young adults believe they can become whatever they want to be and do not wish to acknowledge any limitations. Because of their energy, unbounded enthusiasm and high self-confidence, some do manage truly extraordinary achievements.

To challenge oneself to do better can be a very useful attitude. However, it is even more necessary to recognize what one's body can and cannot do. Whenever we demand of ourselves more than we are capable of accomplishing, we put ourselves at unnecessary risk. Unfortunately, too many young adult males view taking dangerous risks as a way to demonstrate their machismo. To place one's life at risk as a means of demonstrating one's *true masculinity* is not only foolhardy, but also it too often has proven fatal.

The greatest risks to life and limb people face today occur whenever they are in automobiles. Many drivers use excessive speed as a way of saying "I am a powerful person." Turning tight corners at a high speed is often viewed as an indication of male virility. Games of chicken on the road and showing the *dumb* driver that one will not let them get away with their *stupid* driving tactics leads all too often to injury and death. A number of female drivers now treat their automobiles in a similar fashion and regularly place their own lives at risk.

Far too many people also use their automobiles as instruments to express their aggression. They vent their frustrations of every day life in the ways they drive their cars. Somehow they accept the illusion that being enclosed in an automobile affords protection against the potential counter aggression of the other. Accordingly, they are far too ready and willing to retaliate against what they consider to be personal affronts committed by other drivers. These people seem to believe that they heighten their self-esteem through confrontations on the road. The sad truth is that nothing positive is ever accomplished through such behavior, and far too often injuries occur to these drivers and to other people as well.

We cannot teach another person a lesson when they are not open to learning. This is as true on the open road as it is in all other phases of life. It is indeed unfortunate that many people driving cars should not have a driver's license. However, when we are wise and self-protective, we can steer clear of such motorists rather than attempt to drive them off the road.

All drivers are well familiar with the repeated mantras of *do not drink and drive* and *do not do drugs*. The reason these warnings often fall on deaf ears is many young adults hold a false belief in their own invincibility. Using a designated driver when drinking might be ridiculed as a sign of weakness, for one is not supposed to admit to being weak or out of control. Accordingly, many people dismiss the reality of potential danger by saying *it will never happen to me*.

The same sense of invincibility is responsible for the still large number of people, especially young gay men, who continue to practice unprotected sex despite the prevalence of the AIDS virus. As one enters adulthood, it is natural to feel a strong sense of power; and one is not inclined to think in terms of potential weakness. Coming to terms with personal vulnerability is often the last thing that many young adults are willing to do.

Too often I have seen the lingering and devastating effects the death of a teenager or young adult has upon their peers. When a young friend has actually died, the death challenges false beliefs about invincibility. Subsequently, the survivors often fall into a serious depression after having confronted death, especially one that was needless. Tragic deaths are very disorienting, and many people have a difficult time resolving their reactions and then proceeding with their own lives.

Some people enjoy the rush of adrenalin when they confront potentially dangerous situations. As a result, they flock to such activities. Some people love being scared by movies, or they enjoy the rush of speeding on skis down a hill or parachuting out of an airplane. They gain a sense of mastery and power when they conquer the risks they are taking. I, personally, am in the minority. I have never been drawn to such activities and prefer to avoid an adrenalin rush. Nonetheless, I realize the strong pull one can feel whenever danger is conquered. The difficulty faced resides in those times when the individual does not conquer the danger but rather becomes seriously hurt in the course of its pursuit.

Essentially, it is the wish to prove oneself invincible that leads to unnecessary risk taking with one's physical being. We wish to believe we are all powerful or immortal and, consequently, we behave as if such were the case. Under such conditions, a person is likely not to act in a fundamentally self-protective manner. Too often arrogance is substituted for logical, rational thinking. It is, after all, extraordinarily difficult to accept the truth that we ourselves are fallible and mortal beings.

Risk taking, especially taking unnecessary physical risks, becomes less common for many men as they mature and move from age 20 to 35. During that time many young men become parents and feel a powerful need to be protective of their children. Their strong sense of responsibility makes them realize they must take better care of themselves so that they can attend to the ongoing needs of their children and family.

Taking unnecessary emotional risks is far more common among females than it is among males; but it, too, is a consequence of behaving as if one's wish had indeed come true. Many women wish that the man they recently met will be respectful of them. As a consequence, they do not carefully screen or evaluate this person. By using bad judgment, they might well place themselves at risk for physical abuse or even rape. If the woman believes it is vital for her to have a long-term relationship with a man, her strong desire for the relationship can very well cloud her judgment. In such situations she sees what she wants to see rather than seeing the man for who he actually is. If an individual is too desperate for a partner, the relationship becomes one of unequal power. Exploitation and mistreatment are quite likely to happen when one quickly assumes a dependent role in a relationship.

Again, wish fulfilment drives the behavior pattern. The strong wish to be loved and validated can lead you to abandon reason and logical thinking. As a result, you will be hurt because the lover does not behave in your hoped-for ways. It can be too easy to overlook or deny warning signs whenever we are very needy. In many situations the person really does *know* the truth but is unwilling to face it.

Too many women still maintain the belief they need a man in order to feel important, validated or fulfilled. As a result, they enter into and maintain relationships which are not fulfilling and often prove to be destructive. Mistrust in themselves, and this overinflated valuing of a long-term relationship, can lead to much emotional pain.

In my psychotherapy practice, I have often heard unhappily married women say they were certain they needed their husbands in order to survive. I have heard them describe a typical day: arising at six a.m., cooking breakfast for the husband, driving him to the train station, then returning to prepare the children's breakfast. After driving the children to school, these women tend to all the house chores, iron the husband's shirts, do many necessary repairs, shop and prepare dinner. She then picks up the children from school, supervises their homework, picks up the husband at the train station, serves his dinner and notes that he fell asleep watching TV. This scenario could be repeated for five days of the week, yet such women mistakenly continue to believe they could not function without their husbands. The basic truth in such marriages typically is that the man only offers financial support, which he would have to do whether or not he remained in the marriage. On the other hand, the husband would find life extraordinarily difficult without his wife to take care of many of his basic needs.

We all must learn how to be vigilant and self-protective so we do not place ourselves at risk either physically or emotionally. We need to see the other person as he/she really is. Often that means simply accepting the truth that *what you see is what you get.* We certainly need to risk being vulnerable in order to be able to be loved, but we also need to be able to "see" who that other person really is before placing ourselves in jeopardy. When you effectively make that distinction, it will distinguish necessary from unnecessary risk taking.

Self-Esteem

Very early in our lives we begin to receive feedback from our parents about our behavior. We are rewarded for behaving well, and typically we are reprimanded when we act in ways our parents consider unacceptable. As we mature, we receive more detailed commentary on what we do particularly well and are likely to receive harsh criticism about our shortcomings. We receive this feedback about our behavior from friends, teachers and significant adults. All of these reactions to our behavior lead us to develop a basic sense of our character. This early developed self-concept includes a sense of both our strengths and weaknesses, formed from the views and reactions of other people to our behavior. Even as we approach adulthood, most of us will continue to see ourselves in either a positive or negative light, not because of the present circumstances; rather we retain the same sense of ourselves we acquired when young. The term "self-esteem" refers to the degree to which we either value or devalue ourselves. This level of self-esteem was developed in our early childhood.

People who have high self-esteem consider themselves to be worthwhile individuals and quite capable of succeeding in the different tasks they choose to undertake. When they believe they lack the specific skills required to master an activity, they either avoid initiating the activity or find ways to acquire the necessary skills to be successful. People with low self-esteem do not consider themselves to be very capable. They are reluctant to take risks or to enter into situations with an uncertain outcome. They often hold back from taking chances, and this lack of assertive action makes it very difficult for them to be able to raise their level of self-esteem. On the other hand, people with high self-esteem are likely to continue believing in their capabilities. Their strong sense of self and faith in themselves has typically enabled them to succeed regularly at different endeavors.

Because our basic level of self-esteem is established during childhood and is rarely seriously questioned, people find it difficult to increase their level of self-esteem. Individuals may alter many of their attitudes and behaviors as they mature, but they do not often alter their basic sense of themselves even with acquisition of higher level skills. When people with low self-esteem actually are successful, they often rationalize their successes by attributing them to pure luck. They may tell themselves that others who were impressed with their behavior would change their minds if they really got to know them, etc. Because low self-esteem people do not believe they can be liked for who they are, they often are uncomfortable when they receive warmth and caring. Instead, they believe critical people are the most credible, and they gravitate to relationships with such critics.

Individuals who have high self-esteem function quite differently. They are able to independently and rationally evaluate those who evaluate them. As a result, they are capable of deciding when the feedback is helpful and valid, and they can also determine when feedback is biased and should not be trusted.

Even though we are all processes of change, most of us do not alter our sense of self to reflect changed behavior in a new situation. Instead, we retain old and inappropriate senses of self which are carried into each new situation. Because one's sense of self and level of self-esteem is primarily based upon early feedback from others, it does not have basic objective validity. Even when we wish to clearly and rationally assess our strengths and weaknesses, it is a truly difficult if not impossible task to accomplish. Our sense of self is too affected by the early feedback we received from others. The basic problem with that early feedback is that very often it was based upon the critic's needs rather than out of a capacity to give fully objective evaluation. For example, tense parents criticize their children for being rowdy and aggressive when, in fact, it is the parents' own tension level causing this hypercritical response.

Children who receive a great deal of negative reactions from parents are, therefore, likely to develop low self-esteem. Even though these children long for parental approval and try to do anything in their power to please their parents, in many instances they will fail. Parents who are unhappy, tense or disinterested will continue to find fault with their children and create the conditions under which their children will develop low self-esteem.

As is the case with angry reactions, our expectations are just as crucial in regard to our level of self-esteem. If you have high self-esteem, you set realistic expectations for yourself. You know what to appropriately expect of yourself, and you will usually develop successful behavioral strategies. People with low self-esteem typically use one of two destructive strategies which prevents them from feeling good about themselves. The first technique is to set few expectations or goals in order to avoid potential failure. Unfortunately, this perpetuates the long-standing view of low capability. The other strategy is to set unrealistically high expectations. By demanding too much, this low-esteemed person regularly demonstrates he/she can never truly be successful. The eventual sense of failure is not due to faulty behavior; rather, the failure is caused by setting unrealistic expectations.

In William James' 1890 psychology text, he proposed a simple equation which ingeniously described what constitutes one's level of self-esteem. He said self-esteem could be measured by the number of one's successes divided by the number of one's pretensions. We do not often use the word *pretension* today, but it does convey a particularly useful meaning. By pretensions James was referring to one's total number of expectations. People who have few expectations of themselves will necessarily have high self-esteem because each success will carry a great deal of positive weight.

When self-esteem is measured by James' formula, it becomes apparent that low self-esteem is due to the presence of an unrealistically high number of pretensions. One can be very successful behaviorally and still have low self-esteem if expectations are too high. If one's pretensions demand being a straight A student, committing no social gaffes while being liked by everyone, then that person will necessarily have low self-esteem. Because we humans cannot be perfect and will not succeed in all situations, we will continue to fall short of our expectations. The individual who has a grade point average of 3.9, behaves effectively in an overwhelming proportion of time, and is typically considered a "desirable catch" can still feel like a failure. Why? Because on some rare occasions that person did not behave perfectly, and perfect behavior represents his/her extraordinarily high number of pretensions.

An excellent example of this problem with expectations came out of my therapy practice. An individual consulted me, ostensibly wanting assertion training. Through the course of our discussions it became apparent this particular individual did not really have difficulty in being assertive. Rather, the patient found it intolerable to lose *any* arguments, and this high pretension demanded that winning must occur at all times and at all costs. Such a pretension was the cause of the person's underlying low self-esteem.

There are subtle ways in which our pretensions can affect our thoughts and lead us to feel inadequate. One such self-defeating strategy can be through a *to do* list. In order to be efficient and not forget important chores, many people make lists of what they need to accomplish on any particular day. List making typically is a helpful strategy as long as the list only contains chores that can reasonably be accomplished on that particular day. However, some people write lists containing all they wish they could accomplish on that day. A wish list is very different from a *to do* list. We can never complete the tasks on a wish list in any one day. Accordingly, if you transform a *to do* list into a wish list, you will feel highly stressed as well as inadequate. Perhaps you will label yourself as a failure because you did not accomplish what was on your list. Again, you are being driven by pretensions instead of by realistic and helpful problem solving strategies.

A *to do* list needs to contain the few important things we can reasonably accomplish on a particular day. When the list contains only what can be satisfactorily accomplished, one regularly will feel good at the end of the day. It then becomes possible to say "mission accomplished" to yourself and to continue to maintain a high level of self-esteem. When the list is made too long, a person will only feel badly for having fallen short of expectations.

If the nature of one's pretensions is too high, it often feels safer to remain passive and, thereby, avoid a direct failure. If one's pretensions demand never to be rejected for a date or for a job, the best protection is not reaching for anything. If everyone is supposed to find Joe desirable, and in fact many people respond very positively to him, then all Joe has managed to accomplish is simply to satisfy his level of expectation. Such successes cannot be viewed as extraordinary events, given the level of pretensions. If, on the other hand, Joe encounters any kind of disinterest, he may label himself a failure for failing to meet his expectations.

Therefore, it is very important for all of us to review and re-evaluate the expectations we have of ourselves. Some of these expectations may be better defined as wishes. A large discrepancy should exist between what we think *should* happen and what we would *like* to have happen. The discrepancy gives us something to strive for. By changing one's attitude, life becomes much easier and more gratifying because we have raised our level of self-esteem.

A number of years ago I reset my level of expectations and decided I simply wanted to find one good thing about each day. Once that became my expectation (or pretension), I found it quite easy to feel accomplishment. Feeling the warmth of the sun, putting a smile on another's face, or completing a crossword puzzle can be enough good to validate the day. Furthermore, it was easy to discover more than one good thing to cherish about each day. I did not set my expectations too high and, therefore, it was so much easier to relish living. It is, indeed, a wonderful way to feel.

We would benefit if, somehow, we could totally eliminate the dimension of self-esteem from affecting our approach to life. When we redefine ourselves as a process, we realize that what we did yesterday does not have to have any bearing on what we do today. In other words, we may all be quite capable of succeeding at a particular task today, but we may not do as well at a similar task tomorrow. That truth is well know by professional athletes.

Who we are, what we like and dislike can, will and needs to change over time. The old joke "How many psychotherapists do you need to change a lightbulb?" is answered "One, but the light bulb must want to change." When we change our basic definition of ourselves so we see ourselves as a process rather than as a person of either high or low self-esteem, many more opportunities will be present. Good feelings about ourselves become more and more frequent.

Far too many capable people remain trapped by feelings of low self-esteem which were created at an early age but are not logically applicable to their present situations. If we know we are all ongoing processes of change, we are more able to realize the hindrance of carrying these earlier ideas of ourselves into the current moment. We all have *old me's*, and we are all quite capable of being a *new me.* In fact, in order to move ahead with our lives, we need to embrace the possibility of being a *new me.* The *new me* then will also be discarded for still another *new me.* Allowing for these ongoing changes represents both the challenge and the wonderful opportunity to change in gratifying ways.

WORK

According to May (1979), we humans are caught in an inescapable dilemma. On the one hand we are creatures of choice, essentially able to decide what to do or how to be. This capacity to make important choices expresses the side of ourselves May described as being a *subject.* On the other hand, outside forces, people and events can and will affect us, putting us into uncomfortable situations with negative conditions we cannot escape. May stated we are pushed around or victimized by outside forces and at times, we each are nothing more than an *object.* The human dilemma, according to May, is that we are simultaneously *subjects* and *objects.* This condition can be most clearly and graphically demonstrated by noting the struggles people experience in the arena of work.

Virtually all of us must find some kind of employment. We need to survive economically: we need income to put bread on the table and a roof over our heads. The necessity of making money pushes us into the marketplace where either we find a salaried position or become self-employed. In both cases, we cannot avoid being buffeted around as *objects*. When we are salaried, we have to please the boss or the owner of the business and have to conform to the business agenda. If we choose the path of self-employment, we are subject to the conditions of the marketplace, such as when farmers discover a drought can wipe out their savings and result in the loss of the farm. Being in the marketplace means we will essentially be treated as *objects*.

Notwithstanding the fact that we are indeed *objects*, much of what we do at work and how we do it affirms the fact that we are *subjects*. We are at a particular job site because we accepted that job. We chose to pursue one particular career path over another. We, in large, part determine our own success or failure at a job by our degree of investment in our work. We cannot fully control what will happen to us on the job just as we cannot fully control what will happen to us in life. However, we have a certain degree of control over what will happen. For this reason, May (1979) has concluded that we are simultaneously *subjects* and *objects*.

The key to being effective both in and outside the workplace is to become the *subject* or chooser as much as possible and to be the *object* as little as possible. To maximize our power, we need to become better aware of the many forces pushing us into being the victimized *object*. For example, we all know we need to work in order to get money to survive economically. Accepting that reality does not necessarily mean we should direct all of our energies toward making the most money possible. To believe it is imperative to always strive for the highest possible income would place the workplace at the center of one's world. It would mean that other pressures and demands would not be attended to if they interfered with making money. It would be foolhardy to want to fail at work, but we have to decide the amount of importance work has in the larger picture of our personal lives.

The ends of the continuum that describe attitudes toward work are expressed in two basic philosophies. One can *live to work* , or one can *work in order to live.* An individual who adopts the first approach will very likely become a workaholic because personal gratification and basic sense of meaning are all focused upon the workplace. These individuals have narrowed their focus in such a manner that they fail to grow in many personal dimensions.

During late adolescence and early adulthood, most of us found it extraordinarily difficult to choose a career direction. We knew, at least implicitly, that any and all jobs would only utilize a small amount of our skills and interests. If we chose to become a lawyer, for example, we would not have much opportunity for artistic development, to pursue interests in science, or be able to make daily excursions into the great outdoors. Likewise, those who chose scientific research often find few opportunities for working with others in shared collaborative and personal ways. Others who decide to take a job without intellectual challenge may become bored and disinterested in their work.

The choice of any career path means relinquishing so many possible and intriguing kinds of employment opportunities that many people find making such a choice extraordinarily difficult. I believe this struggle is a major reason that many adults spend their 20s making several job changes. They are trying to find gratifying work while struggling with the conformist demands of a workplace which often is bureaucratic, rigid and non-rewarding.

A rough formula once explained how time was allocated over a 24 hour period. One third of the day is spent sleeping, another third at a job, and the remaining eight hours was for a number of routine chores and personal gratification. This formula must have been devised at the time union workers succeeded in reducing the work week to a 40 hour period. Unfortunately, economic conditions often mandate that people spend many more hours at work related activities. Transportation to and from work can take ten or even 20 hours a week.

Professionals are usually expected to devote far more than 40 hours a week toward their work. For many years lawyers have been routinely expected to maintain 60-70 hour work weeks. Physicians during internship work 36 hour shifts, although it has just recently been changed to a maximum of 24 hour shifts and 80 hour work weeks. One would be hard pressed to find a patient wanting treatment from a doctor who had been working nonstop for the past 24 hours.

It is very important to recognize that economics and the marketplace have created conditions which continue to reduce the time people have left for their personal activities and gratification. The concept of true professionalism has almost become transformed into a measure of one's willingness to be overworked. Under such conditions, sensibility has been replaced by exploitation. Corporate America has also adopted these attitudes so that white collar workers are often considered uncommitted and slackers if they only want to work 40 hours a week. When such expectations are rampant, working people are maneuvered into essentially providing free labor to their employers. The unfortunate consequence is a constriction of leisure activities and less time for one's personal life.

When economic conditions made it extraordinarily difficult for families to survive on just one income, women became *liberated* so they could seek employment. It certainly is important for women to have more job opportunities and to develop meaningful careers, but this trend arose from economic necessity rather than a simple reflection of increased personal freedom.

Therefore, in today's economy both married adults may work outside of the home, which raises the stress level for both. When these adults attempt to juggle parenting responsibilities and high job demands, too often they are left with a lack of time for themselves. As a result, a number of people may drift into affairs where they believe they will be more appreciated. High work demands are not alone responsible for a person's level of unhappiness, but they can certainly play an important part in increasing the level of personal distress.

I have conducted my psychotherapy practice in a suburban town where many people commute into a larger city. Some of my therapy clients spend three or more hours every day as commuters. The emotional toll on them has been terrible. This lifestyle only allows a few hours every day to spend with their families. Too often many of them take a few drinks to *settle their nerves* before they feel able to be with their children. When these people decide to seek assistance from a psychotherapist, it unfortunately means they are absent from the home for an additional evening.

Stay-at-home spouses who enter therapy, too, often are very unhappy with the family life style. Wives feel they carry all the responsibilities for the children and for running the home. They also feel it becomes necessary to consistently accommodate their highly-stressed husband's needs; but the husbands often are unable to reciprocate with needed emotional support and understanding. Even with very high incomes, family members can feel neither happy nor fulfilled. Easy acquisition of material possessions is used as justification for their lifestyle, but very often the material goods are insufficient compensation for lack of personal attention.

It is very important to examine one's attitudes, expectations and perspectives about work and to regularly revisit these topics. If you have not yet chosen a particular career path, you need not only consider the type of work you would like but also anticipate the kind of time demands such work will entail. Too often work can dominate people's lives. Their relationships suffer, their children are emotionally neglected, and these workers feel overwhelmed with stress. Life does not have to be that way, and one can avoid making destructive choices leading to such pain.

In considering a possible career choice people need to determine what could possibly make them feel fulfilled, important or satisfied. The career path needs to allow us to express major parts of who we are. You must remember that whatever you choose to do will only draw upon a few of your talents. You must decide which of these talents is the most important to pursue. This choice will not be easy. However, such choices are not immutable, and many people spend their early adulthood changing jobs as they try to determine what career path will be most fulfilling.

If you are currently well into a career path, it still remains important to ask yourself if your work days are meaningful and important and whether they can be improved. If there is little satisfaction at work, it is important to consider possible job or career moves. It is not only *what* we choose to do that can lead to or block a sense of fulfilment, but also *how* we choose to approach our work that will make for either a meaningful or meaningless employment history. High task involvement can produce pride and satisfaction. Disinterest and dissatisfaction will lead to boredom and depression. If you reach a point where you are regularly unhappy with your job, it is crucial to change. It is very important to feel good about yourself; and when the job setting is wrong, you need to fix it. If you find that after changing jobs you still continue to be unhappy, then perhaps you need to consider self-exploration to discover the basic causes of your unhappiness.

Many jobs are routine and offer little intellectual challenge. Consequently, it is easy to be dissatisfied and depressed during such employment. It is important to remember that we are *working in order to live.* We need the paycheck to support our children, take vacations and plan for our future. Persevering with work when the job holds little intrinsic gratification can still be a source of pride. We are making ourselves do what is necessary, and self-discipline is a valuable skill.

We can also find ways of transforming that routine job into something gratifying. We can share with co-workers or perform in such a way to reflect our investment in the tasks. The quality of our work can be viewed as a statement of who we are, so the job performance can be an affirmation of one's self-worth.

Many people believe it is the job itself that causes stress; conversely, it is the workers themselves who generate and produce their personal levels of tension. In many work situations the external demands truly are quite high. However, the way one perceives and responds to these demands either produces ulcers or keeps people free of unnecessary tension. Psychotherapists can fall into the same traps as all other people in this regard.

Several years ago insurance companies decided they would reimburse for only ten therapy sessions per year. People do not really solve their problems in ten sessions, unless the problem is very circumscribed. However, many of my colleagues attempted to complete 40 hours of psychotherapy within a ten session limit. Of course this schedule did not really work, but these therapists were responding to the stress generated by complying to and agreeing with these unreasonable external demands. Nowadays and far too often, the number of psychotherapy sessions people attend are dictated by their insurance policies rather than by their personal psychological needs.

We all have very difficult decisions to make with regard to our interest, dedication and commitment to our places of employment. It is very important to maintain your own perspective and independently decide how much you want to be committed to a job. In work, as in the rest of our lives, each of us can best take care of our needs. We have to manage a difficult balancing act. On the one hand we need to be very task involved so we have a sense of satisfaction and gratification from work. Yet on the other hand, we need to be self-protective and in important ways, remain self-involved enough to attend to our other needs. In your early years of employment it is very easy to work too hard, with too many long hours, particularly because so many jobs demand it. Unfortunately, the people who fall into such a pattern find it quite difficult to change even when the work situation no longer demands it.

When asked to describe what constituted psychological health, Sigmund Freud answered briefly *To love and to work*. Those are simple but still profound sentiments. We humans can certainly love many people and many things for we *know* that such love is an expression of our deep passions. We can also love our work but, hopefully, not with the same level of passion we feel for particular people.

Work is one of the primary ways in which people find meaning. We also find meaning in parenting and in full participation in the world. Because we must spend so much of our lives at work, our career paths need to be personally meaningful and fulfilling. Again, how we handle a particular task is what can make it meaningful and important or, correspondingly, can turn the job and the workplace into a dreary and dreadful experience. We need to make ourselves more the *subject* and as little the *object* in both the workplace and in life.

Uniqueness

A number of years ago an innovative psychologist, Gordon Allport (1961), made some indisputable observations about human personality. He said 1) in some ways all humans are like all other people; 2) in some ways all humans are like some other people; and 3) in some ways all humans are unique and like no other person. Allport viewed every individual as a combination of each of these three dimensions. He understood that certain people strike us as truly unique but that others do not appear to be very different from most other people. These latter individuals could more readily be understood by studying the characteristics, or common traits, they shared with others. Indeed, some of us relish being very much like John Q. Public while others bask in being their own person.

Nonetheless, there can be no one else who is exactly like you. What you feel, how you feel it, what you think, and what you see are all your own unique experiences of the world. Furthermore, all of us have a history of personal experiences uniquely our own. Other people cannot fully grasp how we feel most of the time although there are times when we feel well understood. Even when another person can understand our experience of the moment, the moment always changes and our experiences change as well. All humans are so enveloped in their own experiences that it is very difficult for anyone to try to suspend one's own experiences in order to completely focus upon understanding the other person. Therefore, we must accept the disorienting truth that we can never fully know another nor can another person fully know us or our experiences.

Because we can never be fully known, it follows that in an important way we will always be alone. This painful truth about our human condition is very difficult to accept. We crave to be understood, empathized with and, most definitely, validated and loved by another. It is certainly true that most of us will be blessed enough to feel validated and loved at some point in our lives. However, because some of our ideas, feelings and experiences will not be known by any other person, we can never be fully loved and validated by another person.

We humans also do not want to have to face our limitations. However much despair we may feel when discovering there are many things we cannot have and much we will not be able to do, we still have the potential to rise above that pain. In fact, by coming to terms with our limitations we become empowered to move forward and to put our own stamp on our lives. Although very difficult, it is probably the most important transformation we will ever undergo.

When we accept the truth that we can never be fully known by another, we will feel some degree of depression because we do not want to be isolated. We are, in the words of Bugenthal (1968), both a part of and apart from others. Of course, we would prefer to be able to choose when we connect and when we do not connect; but we do not want to have to acknowledge that in some ways we will never be fully connected with another.

Yet we have a way to counteract the bad feelings that accompany facing this basic human truth. With much concentrated effort, we all can use our will in order to reduce our level of isolation. We can vow to make ourselves very well known to the people in our lives we consider the most important. We can risk sharing the most meaningful aspects of our experiences with these other people instead of allowing our fear of being criticized, misunderstood or rejected to restrain us. These are the basic messages of this book.

It is ironic that when we accept the inevitability of our human limitations we manage, in some way, to be able to transcend these limitations. Our human condition has inescapable pain, but when we affirm ourselves, despite these limitations, we reach the highest levels of human power. We say, *Although I cannot be fully known, I will become as well known as I can.* We say *I cannot prevent my death from happening, but I can make my life full and meaningful before death happens.* We say *I will necessarily make mistakes and know less than I should know, but I can try as well as I can to reduce my mistakes and attempt to be as informed as is reasonably possible.*

It is tragic that so many people fear if they are well known to others, they will be rejected. Because they succumb to this fear, they prevent themselves from becoming known and, therefore, never receive crucial validation. It is far worse to never become known than it is to encounter certain others who cannot accept you for who you truly are. Being very open about ourselves to others is initially frightening. However, even though we will meet some people who cannot tolerate such direct honesty, there will be others who will flock to us because they find our openness very appealing.

Openness and honesty typically generate more openness and honesty from other people. In those very rare instances where openness does result in rejection, it is preferable to quickly acknowledge that the other person does not like you, rather than maintain a non-supportive relationship. We can waste so much time waiting and wondering *what if.* It is easier and better not to wait but simply to find out where others stand: be open and direct with them.

I advocate that we all take the risk of being fully open in relationships because life is too short to waste time. It is only through risk taking that we make important things happen. Passivity is the non-affirmation of the self. When we are active and direct with others, we affirm who we are and, more importantly, who we are becoming. A definite way to lose is not to take chances because of fear. Certainly it is true that sometimes you lose when you take a chance. However, directness succeeds far more often than it produces failure. Furthermore, not making a choice is still a choice.

Of course, I am against automatic conformity; instead I advocate the further development of our uniqueness. Initially it may seem easier to dress like everyone else, drink like everyone else, act like everyone else and not put yourself at risk. But such actions are essentially escapes from living rather than affirmations of being.

My doctoral dissertation drew upon the psychological theory of games. The theory of games essentially speaks about the different strategies people use in making life choices. One can use a *minimax* strategy which means we act in such a way as to minimize our maximum loss. For example, such people decide to place their savings in an insured bank account because they are guaranteed by the federal government never to lose the money. The amount of interest earned on this money will be smaller than the potential return received on other investments. However, through such a strategy they are able to avoid risk. These kind of choices embody what is meant by a *minimax* strategy.

On the other hand, a person can engage in a *maximin* strategy in which he/she attempts to maximize minimum gain. Those following this strategy would regularly buy many lottery tickets and whenever making investments, would be attracted to risky situations that might produce very high rewards. The person who lives using a *minimax* strategy takes as few risks as possible because losing is too painful. The person who lives using a *maximin* strategy can tolerate loss because the most important thing for them is to obtain the largest possible win.

Each strategy is useful in particular limited situations, but it would not be wise to adopt one of these strategies as a basic life plan. We need to take some risks, but we also need to be self-protective. Individuals classified as conformists can be described as progressing through life by adopting a *minimax* strategy. They fear there is much to be lost by letting others know their private thoughts and their private selves. Many people who choose to be conformists feel so much pain from rejection that they never again place themselves at risk. By choosing to avoid pain, they also choose to block off the possibility of deeper satisfaction and fulfilment.

Choosing a *minimax* strategy again points out the dilemma we humans invariably face. We cannot have pleasure without also opening ourselves to pain. We cannot fully love without allowing ourselves to deeply hate. We cannot make a good choice without having previously made bad choices. In other words, we can know or experience one thing only because we know and experience its opposite. Such is the nature of dialectic reasoning. Coming to terms with this most difficult aspect of dialectical reasoning is very empowering for us all.

We all need to face this truth: we can never fully know what will happen or when it will happen. As Tillich (1960) states, the ultimate manifestation of that ignorance is that we cannot fully know about our impending death. Our death is where we will be the ultimate victims, and we can do nothing about it. We also can never fully know the right course of action, which means that, at times, we will make wrong choices and feel guilty. We also can never be fully affirmed by another person, which leads to our fear that we may live a meaningless existence. All of these are very painful truths.

Nonetheless, knowing of eventual death enables us to transform our lives into the highest form of self-affirmation. Knowing that we can never fully *know* what is right enables us to reason carefully and not act impulsively in order to be as correct as possible. Knowing that we cannot be fully affirmed makes us recognize we want to be as fully known as possible. All of these decisions are choices that come out of the use of our will. Through our will we are truly recreating ourselves.

Using our will to move forward in life is the highest form of self-affirmation. In so doing, our lives will be the fullest expression of the singular and unique beings we are and who we can become. The more that each of us trusts in the process of being, the more creative and interesting people we will become. As we continue with our own personal development, we will touch many lives and be loved by others as well. The more fully we trust in ourselves, the quicker we move toward *becoming plumb healthy*.

References

Adler, A. (1968). *The practice and theory of individual psychology*. Totowa, NJ: Littlefield, Adams & Co.

Adorno, T. W., Frenkel-Brunswik, Else, Levinson, D. J., & Sanford, R.N. *(1950). The authoritarian personality.* New York: Harper.

Allport, G.W. (1960). *Becoming: Basic considerations for a psychology of individual personality.* New Haven, CT: Yale University Press.

Boss, M. (1963). *Psychoanalysis and daseinanalysis.* New York: Basic Books Inc.

Bugenthal, J.F.T. (1965). *The search for authenticity.* New York: Holt, Rinehart & Winston.

Camus, A. (1993). *The plague.* New York: Alfred A. Knopf Inc.

Frankl, V. (1960). *The doctor and the soul.* New York: Alfred A. Knopf Inc.

Frankl, V.(1960). *Man's search for meaning: An introduction to logotherapy.* New York: Pocket Books.

Fromm, E. (1941). *Escape from freedom.* New York: Farrar and Rinehart.

Fromm, E. (1955). *The sane society.* New York: Rinehart & Co. Inc.

Hawthorne, N. (2000). *The scarlet letter.* New York: Modern Library.

James, W. (1890). *The principles of psychology.* New York: Dover Publications Inc.

Jasper, K. (1955). *Reason and existenz: Five lectures.* (W. Earle, Trans.) New York: Noonday.

Kierkegaard, S. (1957). *The concept of dread.* (2nd ed.) (W. Lowrie Trans.) Princeton, NJ:Princeton University Press.

Maslow, A. (1954). *Motivation and personality.* New York: Harper.

May, R. (1977). *The meaning of anxiety* (rev. ed.). New York: W.W. Norton & Co. Inc.

May, R. (1979). *Psychology and the human dilemma.* New York: W.W. Norton & Co. Inc.

Pollan, M. (2001). *The botany of desire: A plant's view of the world.* New York: Random House.

Potash, H.M. (1979). *Inside clinical psychology: A handbook for graduate students and interns.* Madison, NJ: Gordon Handwerk.

Potash, H.M.(1994). *Pragmatic-existential psychotherapy with personality disorders.* Madison, NJ: Gordon Handwerk.

Rank, O. (1968). *Will therapy and truth and reality.* New York: Alfred A. Knopf Inc.

Rogers, C.R. (1951). *Client-centered therapy.* Boston: Houghton Mifflin Co.

Rokeach, M. (1960). *The open and closed mind.* New York: Basic Books.

Sartre, J.P. (1956). *Being and nothingness.* (H.E. Barnes, Trans) New York: The Philosophical Library.

Sartre, J. P. (1943). No exit and the flies. New York: Knopf.

Sheldrake, R. (2000). *Dogs that know when their owners are coming home: and other unexplained powers of animals.* New York: Crown Publishing.

Sullivan, H.S. (1953). *The interpersonal theory of psychiatry.* New York: W.W. Norton & Co. Inc.

Tillich, P. (1952). *The courage to be.* New Haven, CT: Yale University Press.

Webster's new world dictionary of the english language. (1957). Cleveland & New York: World Publishing Co.

Herbert M. Potash is Professor Emeritus at Fairleigh Dickinson University where he directed the master's programs in psychology, training many clinical psychologists. He maintains a psychotherapy practice and also supervises mental health professionals. Previous books are *Inside Clinical Psychology: A Handbook for Graduate Students and Interns*; and *Pragmatic Existential Psychotherapy With Personality Disorders*. He has made countless presentations and written numerous articles for professional journals.

He lives in New Jersey with his wife and two Welsh terriers and enjoys yoga, tap dancing and gardening.

For additional orders or e-book requests, please visit our website at **www.gordonhandwerk.com**